Andrew McDeere

BACKYARD CHICKENS and BEEKEEPING

For Beginners

A Complete Step by Step Illustrated Guide to Raise Chickens and your First Bee Colony

Copyright © 2020 publishing.

All rights reserved.

Andrew McDeere

No part of this publication may be reproduced, distributed or transmitted in any form or by any means, including photocopying recording or other electronic or mechanical methods or by any information storage and retrieval system without the prior written permission of the publisher, except in the case of brief quotation embodies in critical reviews and certain other non-commercial uses permitted by copyright law.

Table of Contents "Backyard Chickens"

- **INTRODUCTION**
- Definition of 'poultry.'
- **BEGINNER'S GUIDE TO RAISING BACKYARD**
- Starting Out Q&A
- Planning and Buying Your Chickens
- Financial Statements
- How Many Chickens Should I Get?
- Where Do I Get My Chicks?
- What Should I Look Out For?
- Chicken Coops 101
- Basic Shelter Requirements
- Adequate Amount of Space
- Temperature Control
- Nesting Boxes
- Roosts
- Outside Roaming/Pen
- Security
- **HOW TO RAISE CHICKS**
- Brooding Box
- Bedding
- Warmth
- Food
- Water
- Hygiene
- Security
- **HOW TO RAISE CHICKENS**
- Water
- Food
- Hen Morning and Evening Routines

- Common Chicken Problems
- Molting
- Stopped Egg Laying
- Reasons Why Your Chickens Stopped Laying Eggs
- Broodiness
- What Exactly Is A Broody Hen And How To Stop It?
- What Is A Broody Hen?
- How to Stop a Broody Hen?
- BEST BEGINNER CHICKEN BREEDS
- Why Do You Want Chickens?
- Typical Chicken Characteristics Beginners Look For
- BEST EGG LAYING CHICKEN BREEDS
- SURPRISING RULES FOR FEEDING CHICKENS
- What Should You Feed Chickens?
- How to Feed chickens
- How much are you supposed to feed them?
- Water for Your Hens
- Feeding Chickens Table Scraps
- 5 Healthy Treats
- What you Shouldn't Feed Them
- What Can Happen if Their Diet Isn't Right?
- TOP 13 BEST EGG LAYING CHICKEN BREEDS 55
- WHAT TIME DO HENS USUALLY LAY?
- HOW COLD IS TOO COLD FOR BACKYARD CHICKENS
- Signs of Cold Weather Stress
- A Well Designed Coop
- What About Sick or Injured Chickens and the Cold Weather?
- Keeping the Drinking Water from Freezing
- How Cold is Too Cold for Backyard Chickens?
- THE MOST RARE CHICKEN BREEDS
- Dong Tao

- Ayam Cemani
- History
- GENERAL
- GROOMING
- DIET OR NUTRITION
- SOCIALIZING THE BIRD
- Onagadori
- Polverara
- Ixworth
- Naked Neck
- Golden Campine
- Where To Find These Birds To Add To Your Flock
- CARING FOR THE BIRD(s)
- GENERAL
- GROOMING 98
- DIET AND NUTRITION
- SOCIALIZING THE BIRD(s)
- Vorwerk
- Modern Game
- HISTORY
- TAKING CARE OF YOUR CHICKEN FLOCK
- Vaccinations
- De-worming
- Types of worms:
- Tapeworm
- Gapeworm
- Round-Worm
- TAKING CARE OF YOUR FLOCK
- Mites:
- Lice:
- Fleas

- Ticks
- Bathing your chickens
- Clipping nails
- Clipping wings
- Dust baths
- The hot summer months
- The colder winter months
- Foraging
- Once a month
- Each six months
- Once a year
- **CONCLUSION**

Table of Contents "Beekeeping"

- **INTRODUCTION**
- **WHAT IS BEE STOCK? A SUBSPECIES OF APIS MELLIFERA?**
- **THINGS TO CONSIDER WHEN DECIDING ON A BEE STOCK**
- **THE MAIN SUBSPECIES OF HONEY BEES (APIS MELLIFERA)**
- **BEGINNER BEEKEEPING STEPS WITH A TOP BAR BEE HIVE**
- **WHAT HIVE TOOLS DO I NEED FOR WORKING WITH MY BEE HIVE?**
- **PEST CONTROL**
- **HONEY COLLECTION**
- **HONEY BEES FOR SALE**
- **A FEW POINTS TO CONSIDER BEFORE YOU BUY**
- **WHERE TO GET BEES**
- **FEEDING HONEY BEES FOR BEGINNERS**
- **WHAT TO FEED BEEN IN THE HIVE**
- **HONEY AS FEED FOR BEES**
- **MAKING AND FEEDING SUGAR SYRUP**
- **BEEKEEPING KITS WITH JAR FEEDERS**

- **FEEDING SUGAR WATER IN WINTER – NO**
- **HONEY BEE SWARMING**
- **COLD TEMPERATURE AND HONEY BEES**
- **HOW LONG DO HONEY BEES LIVE?**
- **HOW ARE QUEEN HONEY BEES DIFFERENT FROM WORKERS?**
- **HOW LONG DO BEES LIVE?' AND THE LIFE CYCLE OF BEES**
- **WHAT TO DO TO REVIVE BEE**
- **URBAN BEEKEEPING**
- **WHEN HARVESTING HONEY-TIPS & TRICKS**
- **HOW DO YOU INSPECT THE QUALITY OF honey AT HOME?**
- **HOW TO ATTRACT HONEY BEE TO YOUR EMPTY HIVE (BAIT)**
- **HOW ARE YOU ENCOURAGING BEES TO CONSTRUCT A COMB?**
- **5 TIPS FOR MAKING HONEYCOMB BEES**
- **WARRE HIVE**

Andrew McDeere – Rosanne Fox

BACKYARD CHICKENS

For beginners

> "The Essential Backyard Chickens Guide for Beginners: Choosing the Right Breed, Raising Chickens, Feeding, Care, and Troubleshooting."

Copyright © 2019 publishing.

All rights reserved.

Andrew McDeere

No part of this publication may be reproduced, distributed or transmitted in any form or by any means, including photocopying recording or other electronic or mechanical methods or by any information storage and retrieval system without the prior written permission of the publisher, except in the case of brief quotation embodies in critical reviews and certain other non-commercial uses permitted by copyright law.

INTRODUCTION

Raising backyard poultry can be rewarding not only for the production of consumable eggs and meat but also for companionship and personal pleasure. Providing veterinary care to these clients and their birds can be equally rewarding as long as the veterinarian has a strong understanding of federal, state, and local laws and regulations that affect backyard poultry and has a working knowledge of common diseases and treatments for these species.

Definition of 'poultry.'

The word 'poultry' should be treated as referring to any avian species that has the capacity for its meat, eggs, or other sections (e.g., offal, feathers, manure) to join, directly or indirectly in the human food chain, regardless of the actual use of individual birds of each species. The Code of Federal Regulations (CFR) describes 'major' animal species like dogs, cats, horses, goats, pigs, chickens, and turkeys. All others are known to be "minor" animal species, such as ducks, geese, game birds, pigeons, etc. Demographics It is widely recognized that backyard poultry is growing in popularity. This is not shocking, considering the national trend towards locally produced food and organic food. Poultry breeding can also be socially enriching and instructional. According to the U.S. Department of Agriculture (USDA) National Animal Health Monitoring System (NAHMS) Poultry 2010 study "Urban Chicken Ownership in Four U.S. Cities," which surveyed urban chicken ownership in Chicago, Los Angeles, Houston, and New York City, 0.8% of all households in these cities owned chickens and 4.3% owned single-family homes on one acre or more. About 4 percent of households that did not have chickens at the time of the study were planning to own chickens in the next five years. With the recent steady decline in parrot possession, there is no question that poultry veterinary patients will become more prominent in the coming years.

Birds The majority of poultry birds fall within a few avian orders, including Galliformes (e.g., chickens, turkeys, quail, pheasants, grouse, and guinea fowl), Anseriformes (ducks, geese, swans) and Columbiformes (pigeons and doves). Ratites such as ostrich and emus should also be regarded as poultry animals. Storey's Illustrated Guide to Poultry Types 2007 is an excellent resource for learning about different types of poultry.

Domestic chicken, Gallus domesticus, is widely believed to be a descendant of red jungle birds from geographical areas such as southern China and Indonesia. At the same time, genetic cross-breeding may have occurred with other avian species, such as gray and Sri Lankan jungle birds. Currently, there are hundreds of chicken types around the world, classified by category (geographical area (e.g., American) and, for bantams, by physical traits such as Single Comb), variation (based on physical characteristics such as color and comb type), and stress. Chickens are often categorized as regular breeds (usually larger and more common and commercially bred for eggs and meat such as bared rocks or Rhode Island Reds), bantam breeds (smaller breeds such as silkies) and heritage breeds. Consumer varieties shall contain broilers and plates. See American Poultry Association Perfection Guidelines (http:/www.amerpoultryassn.com) for more information about chicken breeds.

Regulation and biosecurity Plant laws and regulations. Although the commercial poultry industry is tightly regulated by federal and state legislation, poultry in the backyard is generally excluded. Regulation of backyard poultry flocks is usually limited to local regulations, and some municipalities do not have any regulations at all. Local regulations may regulate ownership by requiring permits or licenses, or by dictating care and husbandry, such as defining limits on the size of the property and the available coop space per bird, and through the noise, odor and cleanliness nuisance clauses.

Biosafety or quarantine; Note that "an ounce of prevention is worth a pound of cure." Biosafety is the cheapest and most effective way of restricting and stopping the introduction and dissemination of infectious agents to and within a backyard flock. There are three main biosecurity principles: access management (e.g., closed definition of the flock, enclosure, and confinement), animal health management (e.g., good record-keeping, veterinary care) and environmental management (e.g., sanitation or disinfection, pest control).

Backyard poultry inherently poses a risk to the commercial poultry industry for the spread of highly pathogenic diseases such as exotic Newcastle disease (END) and highly pathogenic avian influenza (HPAI). The vet plays a key role in the early detection and notification (reporting) of potentially serious contagious diseases.

BEGINNER'S GUIDE TO RAISING BACKYARD

Chickens Raising chickens can be a lot of stuff: relaxing, satisfying, enjoyable, and for beginners, maybe a little anxious!

There are tons of information on raising chickens and chicks, and it's hard to sort through it all to find out what's true, what's wrong, and what's odd.

In this definitive guide, I've brought everything together

Starting Out Q&A

Before you get your chickens or chicks, you need to ask yourself a few questions: why are you raising them? Eggs, meat, or pleasure?

- Where are you going to get them?
- Are you prepared to spend some time with them?
- Are you able to' muck out' their coop when it's needed?
- Who's going to take care of them if you go on vacation?
- Are you allowed to have chickens, if so, how many?
- Such questions could be

Choosing the Best Breed of Chicken Here, in the twenty-first century, we have a beautiful selection of chickens to choose from.

How many different races are there?

No-one really knows, but it's estimated to be in the hundreds. There are birds that have been specifically bred for enhanced egg laying, quality meat, fights, and plumage.

While there are several numbers of chicken varieties,

It's wrong! Unfortunately, you're going to be disappointed if you want egg layers and have bought a bunch of Sultan chicks because they look pretty. They're going to lay an egg a week if you're lucky!

Planning and Buying Your Chickens

It's time to take the plunge! You want chickens, and you know which breed you want, but you're not sure where to start.

For the first time, when you get chickens, you have a couple of different choices.

We will look at the good and the bad of each option. You can buy hatching eggs, chicks, poles, or adult birds. Each choice has its merits, but it's really about what you think is best for you.

Financial Statements

Hatching Eggs: These are fertilized eggs that <u>you</u> need to incubate. If you are new to chickens, I don't recommend that you get hatching eggs unless you really know what you are doing. Although incubation is fairly straight forward, there's definitely an art to it.

Chicks: This is the most used and wise choice for novices. You can select which breed(s) you want and when you want them. You typically get chicks at one day old.

Pullets: Pullets are birds aged between four to six months. The chicks have been reared to adulthood, and are usually sold at point of lay, meaning the pullet is about to lay her first egg anytime soon!

Adults: Adult hens are more difficult to come by as breeders like to move birds out before they get too old since they eat more. A common source of adult hens is animal shelters or rescue sanctuaries.

How Many Chickens Should I Get?

You can generally average out how many chicks you will need. If your birds are for eggs only, then you just need to think how many eggs do you use in a week currently?

One hen will average four to five eggs a week. Throw in a couple of extra chicks for 'just in case, and you have your number!

For example, if you want 16 eggs a week, you would need six hens (4 would normally do this many eggs, but I've included 2 'just in case' chicks).

Where Do I Get My Chicks?

The best place for beginners to buy their chickens from is a local farmer, hatchery, or farm supply stores.

Though, if you want to purchase your chickens from further away, the USPS has been shipping chicks for about one hundred years and will ship chicks, which you can purchase online.

What Should I Look Out For?

All birds should have clear, bright eyes. They should be curious about their environment and you. Feathers or fluff should look clean with good coloring. If a bird, regardless of its age, exhibits any of these signs, you should avoid buying it.

- Sleepy, lethargic
- Hunched into a ball
- Sitting by itself
- Reluctant to move
- Any nasal/eye discharge
- Blocked vent
-

Chicken Coops 101

Chickens are not very strict when it comes to housework.

They don't need running water, power, and carpeting. A modified basic wooden box is in a pinch, but there are few crucial things you need for your flock to ensure their safety and well-being.

Basic Shelter Requirements

This is the most important need of all, a spot where they can get out of the blissful heat, howling wind and blowing snow. The coop has to be water-resistant because there's nothing more unpleasant than a wet hen.

Adequate Amount of Space

Adequate habitat for birds to co-exist comfortably is important. If they're crowded together, they're likely to start anti-social behaviors like picking and pecking each other. Winter is the worst season for these behaviors; hens get restless and make trouble.

Temperature Control

Ideally, the coop should be cool in the summer, warm in the winter. Proper ventilation of your coop is important when it comes to temperature control. A good flow of air will keep the coop at an optimum temperature for your hens. You need to install more ventilation holes if you find it's too warm.

Nesting Boxes

For nesting boxes, you'll need about one box for every three hens, but it never hurts to have more. There's always one particular package they're going to squabble over, so more is good.

Roosts

You'll need about one box for every three hens with nesting boxes, but it never hurts to have more. There's always a certain package they're going to squabble over, so more is good.

Outside Roaming/Pen

In addition to a secure coop, your chicken will also need access to some outside space, whether it is contained or free of charge.

Security

A strong and formidable co-op will keep your girls safe at night. Don't imagine, even for a minute, that wolves won't be brazen enough to creep into your yard and try to kill your birds, they're going to, and they're going to do so, with catastrophic results for your birds and heartbreak for you.

HOW TO RAISE CHICKS

Now that you've done your research, and settled on your type, what's going to happen now?

If you've bought them online, the website you've ordered is likely to carry all the items you need to make your kids back.

If you're buying from a farm store, make sure you've got everything you need for the chicks in advance. Farm stores usually sell a large quantity of chick related goods.

Make sure you know what to do; otherwise, you could be parting with hard-earned cash for something you don't want or need.

It helps to break things down into needs and extras, so that's what I've done here for ease of reading.

Brooding Box
This could be as easy as a cardboard box. It's got to be tall enough to stop the chickens from running down. It's got to be big enough for a food dish, a water dish, and chicks.

There is also a need for cold proof drafts that can kill chicks very quickly.

Brooding boxes come in all shapes, sizes, and costs. If you're not sure if you're going to be brooding your chicks again, get the cheapest brooder to start with, you can upgrade yourself later.

Bedding
Something soft like a pine shaving. They are sold in small bales at most farm stores and are affordable.

If your embroiderer box has a sticky floor (like plastic), place some paper towels under the bedding so that they can stay and hold up well; otherwise, they may have trouble standing or moving.

Warmth

Chicks require a lot of energy.

They don't have true feathers until they're around 6-7 weeks old, so they can't regulate their own temperature, so you need to help them.

You can use a heat lamp or heat plate ' Smart chicken.'

They will need to be warmed for about 6-7 weeks or until the ambient temperature is approximately the same as that of the embroiderer.

The temperature at the chick stage will have to be 95F during the first week. This reduces by 5 degrees per week until the ambient temperature is reached.

How do you know if it's warm enough?

If they're all huddled in a group, they're too cold; if they're scattered to the sides of the embroiderer, they're too hot; if they're clustered all over, they're just correct. A thermometer will help you with this too, but base your judgment on the behavior of the chicks.

Food

Chicken food comes in a wide range of choices that can be overwhelming, so here's the scoop. It is advised that you feed your chicks as follows:

- 0-8 weeks: 18-20% starter feed crumbles

- 8-14 weeks: 16-18% starter/grower
- 15-18 weeks: 16% finisher
- 18 weeks upward: 16% layer feed

Chick feed can come as medicated or un-medicated.

Medicated feed is medicated with a coccidiostat that helps protect them from coccidiosis, a terrible disease.

If your chicks have been vaccinated at the source for coccidia, do not use medicated feed.

Chicks are messy; they're going to scratch their food all over the floor, pop in it, and get their bedding in it, so you need a feeder that's going to remove some of that mess.

Before they start eating greens such as short grass and dandelions, they'll need a little chick-grit dish to support digestion and make sure they don't get a seed.

Water

Water is essential to the well-being of all creatures. Chicks are no exception. Water should be at Goldilock's temperature—not too warm, not too cold, but just right.

You're going to have to dip the beak of each chick in the water at first so that they know where it is; after that, they should all be able to find the water dish. Do the same thing with a food dish, too.

If your chicks are only a few days old, you'll need to add some clean pebbles or marbles to the water dish so they can't fall in and drown.

After a week or two, you could cut them because the chicks are going to be strong enough not to sink themselves.

For the first few days, you could apply an electrolyte/vitamin supplement to the water to get them off to a good start.

Change the water frequently (several times a day) as they kick bedding etc. into the water on a regular basis.

Hygiene

Whoever said' cleanness is next to godliness' never kept chickens. I told you that the chicks are messy, so you're going to be the room service for them!

It is very important that their brooder, feeder, and watering area are kept clean. You need to remove the poop daily, change the litter as often as you need it. Once it gets wet, it has to be changed.

Remember, the brooder is very warm, there's poop, and it's wet, it's the perfect breeding ground for bacteria.

Wash and sanitize the feeder and waterer at least every other day. If your chickens are as dirty as mine, you're going to have to throw out a decent amount of food. Once they're pooping in the feeder, the food goes out.

Don't forget, of course, to sanitize and wash your hands before handling food or drinks!

Security

Your brooder full of chicks needs to be safe from wolves, and I also consider house pets as pests.

When you have them in your home, you'll need to make sure that Fido and Fluffy can't get to those little balls of fluff, maybe put them in a separate room or a safe lock on the package.

Seek not to have them in places such as the bathroom, the dining area, and the kitchen. They're stirring up a lot of dirt and dander, people who are allergic to dust may have issues with them at home.

If you're planning to keep the chicks in the outbuilding, you need to be able to exclude any predators; you may have in the area.

Rats, like a chick snack, like foxes, weasels, raccoons, and a host of other carnivorous creatures.

They're going to need you to take intensive care of them until they're around 12 weeks old. Some people say that sooner, but I'm wrong on the cautious side.

Going Outside for the First Time

If you're thinking of putting them out every day for a few hours, you'll need to have something like a dog crate or even a mini-chicken run for them.

Of reality, it's going to have to be animal proof, and that means hawks and owls, as well as digging animals and foxes.

They're going to need a shady area where they can escape from the sun, keep food and water cool.

HOW TO RAISE CHICKENS

So now your chickens have evolved into true chickens!

Managing your adult flock may sound like it's complicated, but it's pretty simple to do. The hen is doing all the job, and you're taking care of her needs. Nonetheless, there are some things you should know before you get confused by hiccups in the process.

Water

Water is essential for all living things, and chickens are no exception.

A hen drinks a cup of water every day. She's going to take frequent small sips all day. Too little water can impact egg production, among many other issues, so make sure they have plenty of water.

There are about 15 cups of water in one US gallon, so if you've got a lot of birds, you'll need a few drinkers for them. As an example, I have about forty birds, and I put out four drinkers in various places to make sure they all have access to water.

You can put the water in any kind of plastic container, but the easiest way is to buy a drinker.

Food

Including water, the other important item chicken wants is food.

Giving the chickens the right food will keep them happy and turn them into an egg-laying unit. If you give them the wrong food, it can lead to all sorts of issues, including abuse and weight loss.

Hen Morning and Evening Routines

Unfortunately, most people live busy lives and don't have to tend their chickens all day.

In the morning, you're going to have to let your chickens out of the coop, check on their food and water, and take a general look around and make sure everyone's ok.

It's time to start the evening routine when the sun comes down. This will include, safely lock the girls inside the coop and also collect eggs (if you haven't already done so).

For example, this is the sweet minimum of caring for your women. There will also be regular activities, such as washing the coop and tending the nesting boxes.

Common Chicken Problems

Unfortunately, at some stage in the life of your chickens, they're likely to have some kind of concern, whether it's broodiness, pests, or abuse.

There are a number of common problems that occur when you have chickens. If you're not ready for them, they may seem intimidating and daunting.

Molting

Molting is the process of losing all old, worn-out feathers and replacing them with new plumage. It's going to happen to all birds, including roosters. Some birds may take up to two years to complete a molt, but a humble chicken is usually done in three months.

Reasons Why Your Chickens Stopped Laying Eggs

There are lots of reasons why the chickens might have stopped laying, but you don't need to rush out and buy supermarket eggs right now!

Today, we're going to look at the most common reasons that your chickens have stopped laying and what you can do to get them laid again.

1. Their food: The most common reason why the chickens quit laying is that there's something wrong with their diet. Have you recently changed your diet or even changed the brand of pellets that you feed to your chickens?

We once decided to stop feeding our chickens with layers of pellets and instead feed them with maize. Maize is just ground the corn.

When feeding the girls layers of pellets, we were getting an average of 9 eggs a day, and after feeding them Maize for a matter of days, we were only getting 4-5 eggs a day!

Yikes- This is because maize does not contain a lot of protein, so chickens require about 20 grams of protein every day to keep laying eggs.

Just note, whatever you feed your chickens, they need a well-balanced diet to make sure their bodies are capable of producing eggs.

If you're feeding your girls loads of pellets and they're still unable to lay down, consider giving them protein-rich foods such as pumpkin seeds, oats, and mealworms.

Water is another often overlooked aspect of their diet. When chickens don't have access to fresh water all day, you can say goodbye to your eggs.

2. Not Enough Daylight: So you've made sure your girls get plenty of protein and fresh water, but there's still no eggs in sight. Sometimes, it could just be the wrong time of the year for your hens to lie down.

Your chickens need plenty of natural daylight to lay eggs-at least 14 hours a day and 16 hours is even better.

This means that during the winter, when in the US, natural daylight can drop to less than 9 hours a day, your girls would need another 5 hours of daylight to lay eggs.

The solution is to place an artificial light in their coop and set it to an automated timer. This will certainly keep the egg production up, but it's something we're not going to do.

There's a reason why hens don't lay as much in the winter, and their body needs to rest and recover for the next year. And if you don't give them time to recover their bodies, you'll do more harm than good in the long run.

It's not all bad news though, the chickens aren't supposed to stop laying entirely, and you're supposed to get the odd eggs, but that's it.

3. Broody Hens: So your girls are well fed, getting plenty of sunlight, but they're not laying down yet. It's time to give them up and get a new herd, just a joke!

You might have a brooded hen, and in this case, she won't lay eggs, no matter how much protein or sunshine you give her.

When a hen gets tangled, she needs to hatch her own chickens, so she's going to sit on top of her eggs for 21 days before they hatch. During this 21 day cycle, she won't lay any eggs, not good. There are clear signs to look out for if your hen is bridal: she'll be sitting in the nest box all day.

She's going to become very protective and prevent anything from getting close to her nest.

She's going to remove her breast feathers to heat the eggs out of her body.

When you think your hen is bridal, learn how to avoid my bridal chicken.

4. New additions to the flock: So you don't have a broody hen, but you still don't see any eggs. Have you recently moved your chickens or introduced new chickens to the flock?

Chickens enjoy routine, and the slightest disruption in their schedule usually results in their laid off.

The most frequent daily disturbance they undergo is when they're relocated. This could be when they're delivered to your home after you've bought them, or when you've decided to move their coop.

Chances are that you purchased your chickens as pullets, so they weren't feeding before they came anyway. But if you moved their coop, they're not going to be happy with you!

Give them a couple of days to get around, and they're supposed to start laying again.

If you've just introduced new chickens to the flock, this can also disrupt their routine and egg-laying. When new chickens are introduced, there tends to be some shoving and jostling for the first few days when a new pecking order is established. During this time, they're not going to lay eggs, but again, after a few days, they're going to start laying again.

5. Some Breeds Don't Lay As Many Eggs: Other breeds just don't lay as well as others, and we sometimes forget that, particularly when we hear about how large other people's eggs are.

Breeds such as Rhode Island Reds or Buff Orpingtons may lay more than 200 eggs per year. Whereas other species, such as Ameraucanas and Silkies, are known to lay fewer than 100 eggs per year.

If you're unsure how many eggs your chicken breed should lay every year, this beginner's guide to chicken breeds should help.

6. Old Age: So you have a Red Rhode Island, which is supposed to lay more than 200 eggs a year, and they've just stopped laying.

Unfortunately, as chickens grow older, the amount of eggs they lay slows down. Look at the picture below, and you can see that you normally only get about three years of good chicken egg-laying.

If your Rhode Island Red had laid 200 eggs in their first year, they would have laid around 168 eggs in their second year, 128 eggs in their third year. This number will continue to fall to around 40 eggs in the tenth year.

If your chickens get a little older, then a drop in egg laying is perfectly natural and expected.

There's nothing you can do about it, and it's just nature's way when the chickens mature.

7. Illness: If you have a well-fed, well-established young chicken, it has plenty of natural daylight, and they suddenly stopped laying, there's the possibility that they're ill.

Colds: signs to watch out for are slimy eyes, and they're running around with their beak open, so they can't breathe through their ears. Make sure you isolate any chicken you think might have a cold so that it doesn't spread to the rest of the flock.

Parasites: contain lice, mites, and worms. You'll notice your chickens are going pale, and they're not going to stop itching themselves. The easiest way to treat any parasite is to spray chicken coops and chickens with a chicken cleaner. Something like Johnson's Poultry Housing spray is supposed to do the trick.

Molts: A lot of people misinterpret the signs above as a virus when it's just chicken molding. Chickens mulch each year, and it may take about 6 to 12 weeks for them to grow new feathers, they will not lay eggs during this time period.

If you want to keep track of how many eggs your chicken has laid, this spreadsheet should help. You can either fill it in or print it off on your desktop or stick it up elsewhere.

Broodiness

What's a bridal hen? You're going to know when you see it! She's going to sit in the nest all the way. If anyone comes near her, she's going to grumble, squawk, and puff herself out. Maybe she's going to give you an all-powerful cock too. What's a broody hen, and how to avoid it?

What Exactly Is A Broody Hen And How To Stop It?

Your hen squawks each time you touch her, and she doesn't leave her nesting box, what's up, is she sick? Far from it, and the odds are that she's just bridal and wants chickens. If you're not planning to have chicks, this can be problematic because the hen in question will stop laying eggs.

Whatever is the case, you can be sure that if you want chicks and need a bridal hen, there won't be one in sight, but the day you don't want a bridal hen, it's the day you will see one!

Let's take a look at how to spot a bridal hen and want you to do something to keep her from being bridal.

What Is A Broody Hen?

The broody hen is a hen that needs their eggs to hatch. She's going to sit on top of her eggs (and others she's stolen) all day long trying to hatch them. Obviously, if there's no rooster involved, the eggs won't be viable, and for the rest of her life, she can sit on top of the eggs so that they won't hatch!

There is no exact science as to what makes a hen go broody it's a combination of its hormones, instinct, and maturity.

If you've never seen a bridal hen before you might ask, how do you know if a hen is bridal or not? Believe us, once you've seen the signs, you won't have any delusions of becoming a broody hen.

She's going to stay in her nest all day, and we mean, all-day

She's not even going back to roost with the rest of the chickens at night.

She's going to become very territorial about her nest. This means puffing out her wings or squawking at anything that's trying to get near to her.

She's going to peck and try to bite you if you're trying to move around here, so make sure you wear gloves if you need to move her around.

She may also pick out her breast feathers so that the heat from her body passes through to the eggs.

If you want to raise chicks, then having a bridal hen is perfect-after all, it's nature's best incubator. But, if you don't want chickens, it's troublesome to have a bridal duck. Not only will your bridal hen stop laying, but the worst of all, it can cause other hens to turn bridal as well, say goodbye to your egg production!

You could leave her to 'breast,' and after 21 days (which is when the chicks will hatch if the eggs are fertile), she would take advantage of it, but in our experience, they won't, and they need to be 'split.'

So how are you going to break a hen out of her broodiness?

How to Stop a Broody Hen?

The best way to stop a broody hen is because it never happened in the first place, and there are a few things you can do to reduce the chances of your hens becoming broody.

The first thing to do is to remove the eggs from the nesting box as soon as they have been laid. Second, don't let the hens get into the nesting box after the eggs have been laid that day. Now, unless you're around your girls 24/7, both of these options aren't very practical, and you're probably going to find yourself with a bridal hen at some point, so what are you doing?

Well, you've got a lot of options, and you can break her turmoil without causing any emotional damage to her, so don't worry! Let's look at some of the easier options that should work in most situations.

Cut her from her nest box.

Take the broody hen out of her nest, and leave her off with the rest of the chickens in the field. You can do this at the same time as you feed them to maximum effect. Also, as we've already noted, broody hens can bite, so make sure you wear gloves when you do this. Keep an eye on the hen, because she might be going straight back to the nest box. Make this move many times a day to try to destroy it.

Block the nesting box.

She keeps coming back to the nesting box for a few days. It's time to ramp up the ante. Cut her from the nesting box, as you've already done, except once she's out of the nesting box, she's in just hammer a piece of wood to the door. Take the nesting straw out of the package to further dampen her morale just in case she comes back in!

Make her roost again

If she's still bridal, you have a stubborn girl, but don't worry, we still have some more tricks on our sleeves. Just as it's going dark and your hens are going back to the coop to roost, take your broody hen out of her nest and position it with the other chickens roosting. Chances are she won't be bold enough to risk moving back to the nesting box in the night.

Use frozen vegetables

We've always managed to break our hen's broodiness at this point, but other backyard chicken owners haven't been so lucky, so what else can you do? I've heard a few people put a bag of frozen vegetables under their chicken. We do this because, when the hen is brooded, their body temperature increases so that lowering it (with frozen vegetables) often sends a message to their brain that they are no longer brooded.

Bring out the Broody Buster.

I'm sure your hen s no longer bridal at this point. If this is the case, there is one option left, a broody cage! Don't think about it being less exciting than it looks. You'll need a wire bottom cage for this. You can use a dog/cat carrier to take the bottom out and cover it with chicken wire. Make sure there's nothing in the cage except food and water-that means no bedding.

Bullying.

The pecking order is called for a reason. Each bird in a flock will have its own location. Those at the top are the first to eat; those at the bottom are the last to eat. It's a very simple but effective hierarchy, so that all members know their position.

Bullying happens to a small degree every day because of this. If a chicken comes out of turn, she'll get a quick peck to the head to remind her of her status.

Predators.

Even if you live in the middle of the city, there's a chicken predator in your neighborhood. Foxes, coyotes, raccoons, and the baby dog down the road are all going to want chicken dinner, and these are just field animals.

The key to your flock's safety is the safety and awareness of predatory animals and the area in which you live.

BEST BEGINNER CHICKEN BREEDS

Choosing the right chicken breed as a beginner can be the difference between thoroughly enjoying the moment with your chickens and wondering why you ever needed chickens in the first place.

Most people don't know exactly what they want or need when they start looking at the breeds, so that's why we decided to write this article today.

We will address exactly what you need to think about before you decide on your breed, explain what characteristics beginners should look for, and then recommend our top 5 picks for the best egg-laying chicken breeds.

Why Do You Want Chickens?

Before we go any further, we'll ask you a few questions, be sure to either write down your answers or keep them in your head.

First of all, why are you trying to keep chickens? Were you looking to keep chickens for eggs, food, pets, or a mixture of these purposes (though the poultry and pet choices may not go too well together!)?

Many chickens are exceptionally good egg-laying (Rhode Island Reds and Leghorns) and lay a huge number of eggs, while others (Broilers) are ideal for food, but do not lay many eggs.

The next step is to pick the chicken breed you want.

Choosing the right chicken breed as a beginner can be the difference between thoroughly enjoying the moment with your chickens and wondering why you ever needed chickens in the first place.

Many people don't know exactly what they want or need until they start looking at the breeds, so that's why we decided to write this article today.

We will answer just what you need to think about, before you settle on your type, explain what traits beginners can look for, and then suggest our top 5 choices for the best egg-laying chicken breeds.

Why would you like chickens?

Before we go any further, we're going to ask you a few questions, be sure to write down the responses and keep them in your head.

First of all, why do you want chickens to be kept? Are you looking to keep chickens for eggs, meat, pets, or a combination of these reasons (though the meat and pet options probably don't go too well together!)?

Many chickens are exceptionally good egg-laying (Rhode Island Reds and Leghorns) and lay a huge amount of eggs, while others (Broilers) are ideal for food, but do not lay many eggs.

The second question you need to answer is, how much time do you expect to spend with, and take care of, your chickens? Many breeds require a lot of upkeep and effort from you. In comparison, other breeds (such as Buff Orpingtons) are very self-reliant and will not take much effort from you at all.

If you're curious how much time you need to spend with your ducks, read my project here.

Second, you need to care about your climate/weather to make sure it's ideal for the breed you're interested in.

Most of the time, you don't need to worry too much about it, because most breeds will be fine in all climates. Even if the chicken is delivered to you directly, unless the chicken has just been shipped, it will be perfect in your weather. However, if you're buying rare breeds (which we wouldn't recommend to you as a beginner, but more on that later) and you're traveling a long distance to get them, you need to make sure that the climate you're taking is right. Minorca chickens, for example, require very warm climates, so they would not be suitable in certain areas of Russia.

The fourth question you need to think about is how much room do you have for your chickens? Until you respond, make sure you read how much space chicken wants.

Were you planning to keep your chickens in a coop or in a free-range?

Some breeds need more room than others, and if they don't get this room, they can get violent and even start pecking and attacking each other. So make sure you match the breed to what you can offer in terms of roaming space and coop size.

The final question you need to talk about is what your plan is?

Some breeds pay a similar amount per chicken, but more exotic and uncommon varieties can be very pricey, they can potentially cost thousands of dollars.

However, as we discuss later in the article, we would not suggest that beginners buy rare or exotic birds for their first chicken.

Typical Chicken Characteristics Beginners Look For
We've noticed that most of the time, when people contact us wondering what kind of chicken they're supposed to start with, they're all looking for the same thing.

Most beginners are looking for chickens that are easy to keep, lay lots of eggs, are docile, and are not very noisy.

That's why we always recommend starting with what is known as dual-purpose animals. Dual-purpose birds are usually large egg layers, and very calm, we'll discuss specific breeds later on.

Many beginners contact us and inquire about rare breeds and breeds that produce a lot of food. We're not recommending either of these to beginners mainly because they need a lot more time, and they're harder to look after. We also recommend avoiding food or exotic birds until you have more practice.

BEST EGG LAYING CHICKEN BREEDS

So, if you're like us, and you want to start keeping chickens for eggs, which breed would we suggest?

Bear in mind that the ideas below are ideal for people with little experience looking for easy-to-handle backyard chickens, needing little upkeep, and, most importantly, laying a lot of eggs!

1. Rhode Island Red: Rhode Island Reds are associated with chicken keeping in the backyard and one of the most common chicken breeds in the country.

They're friendly, easy to keep, and very tough.

Eggs: should produce more than 250 medium-sized brown eggs per year.

Character: It's very easy to keep, it doesn't take too much room, and it's all year round.

2. Animal dogs, such as Golden Comets, have been bred to eat small amounts of food and lay as many eggs as possible. While this is good for you, it can hurt the hen's wellbeing because their body rarely rests.

Eggs: upwards of 280, medium-sized, brown eggs per year.

Character: Hybrids tend to make excellent surfaces, eat less meat, and are not likely to be broody. We make a great selection, just make sure you get your cross from a responsible breeder and make sure it's not over-bred.

3. Buff Orpington is one of the simplest and most common egg-laying chickens in the world. They reside from Kent, England, and are known for their good looks and sturdiness.

Eggs: should be produced at least 180 medium-sized, light brown eggs per year.

Character: Orpington makes great pets, as they are extremely friendly and soft. However, they do get broody during the summer months, so their egg production is slightly lower than some of the other breeds mentioned here.

4. Plymouth Rock, also known as barred rocks, originates from the USA and is one of the most popular dual-purpose chickens.

Eggs: are expected to produce 200 medium-sized brown eggs per year, which are also laid during the winter.

Character: A very friendly bird that performs best as a free-range and makes a perfect backyard hen. They're also extremely friendly to people, so good that you want to teach them to feed from your side!

5. Leghorn The Leghorn breed originated from Italy and was first imported to the USA in the 1800s. They don't get broody sometimes, and they're the perfect choice for year-round egg-laying.

Eggs: should produce more than 250 medium-sized white eggs per year.

Character: Leghorns will be great in the gardens as they are a very healthy bird, but they are not very tame, so they are not ideal for people with children who want them as a shelter.

With these recommendations, it is important to remember that you always get bad-chickens, and even the most docile breed will sometimes produce troublesome birds.

All of these breeds above should be available from the local hatchery, and at the beginning, we would recommend that you do not mix breeds within your flock.

Pick a breed and start with it. This will help to reduce pests and stop them from attacking each other.

SURPRISING RULES FOR FEEDING CHICKENS

Feeding your chickens is one of the most important tasks, if not the most important task when it comes to raising chickens in the backyard. Get it wrong, and you'll have a safe flock that is ready to cluck every time you bring them one of their favorite snacks or kitchen scraps!

Get it right, and it can lead to reduced egg production, deformed eggs, feather harvesting, and other undesirable behavior.

Now, let's get right into all you need to know about feeding chickens.

What Should You Feed Chickens?

Once you know what you're doing, feeding your chickens is going straight ahead. We think what makes this tricky are some of the unfounded assumptions posted online about what you can and can't feed your chickens (such as feeding your chickens potato skin is terrible for them, that's right! Chickens love potato skin).

A high-quality poultry pellet is the basis of any good chicken diet.

We feed our girls layers of pellets that give them the perfect amount of protein and minerals to stop them from laying eggs! Pellets usually contain wheat, salt, maize, sunflower seed, and oats.

Feeding your chickens pellets means that essential vitamins, nutrients, and minerals enter their food source to keep them healthy. This is even more important if your girls don't have much outdoor space because they're not going to be able to get minerals and salt from the ground.

In contrast to their simple pellet diet, you can feed them grains such as corn and wheat to give them some kind of choice.

Chickens like fruit and vegetables, and you can bring them this every day. The girls love potato peels, bananas, tomatoes, carrots, and broccoli. You are safe to feed chickens almost any vegetable or fruit except raw green peels (such as green potato peel) and any citric fruits such as oranges and lemons.

Only note that they need whole wheat, low salt, and low sugar meat.

Hens are healthy, and eggs are laid. We listed some of our favorite feeds in the table below.

How to Feed chickens

So now you know what you're supposed to feed your birds, the next question is how you're going to feed them?

Once in the morning and once in the evening, we feed our chickens pellets, remember that they like to eat small portions, but often.

Most people prefer to throw chicken pellets down on the ground and let their chickens hold to it. We put our pellets in a chicken trough to keep them clean and dry.

How much are you supposed to feed them?

Generally, free-range chickens won't eat anymore, so you can't force them. If you put too many pellets in their feeder, they just won't eat them.

Be careful not to leave any pellets or feed overnight, because it will attract pests such as mice.

Through time, you'll learn exactly how much feed your chickens require, and this will depend on the breed, how busy they are, and the time of year. If you are constantly finding feed in the trough, reduce the amount you give them slightly.

We've got 12 models, and we found out that every morning and evening, four-wide handcuffs keep them happy.

Interesting side notes: A hen requires approximately 4 pounds of chicken feed to produce 12 eggs (source).

How often are you supposed to feed them?

This is going to depend more on the situation than on the chickens. If you're unemployed and spend most of your time at home, you can feed them many times during the day.

Though, if you're busy and away from home all day, you're better to feed them once in the morning and then again in the evening when you're back home.

Another thing to keep an eye on while you're feeding them is to make sure the most aggressive (remember our pecking order discussion?)

hens don't eat all the meat. If this is becoming an issue, consider feeding the weaker birds on their own to make sure they get some food.

Water for Your Hens

Providing your hens with water is very straight ahead, you just need to make sure they have access to clean, fresh water at all times.

You can put the water in any kind of plastic container, but the easiest way is to buy a drinker.

During the winter, when you stay in a colder climate, the water is likely to freeze in the evenings, so make sure you break the ice and wash the tank in the mornings.

Feeding Chickens Table Scraps

Of example, no chicken feeding conversation is complete without thinking about table/kitchen scraps.

One of the many benefits of keeping chickens is that the vast majority of your kitchen waste can be cooked. It means they're going to get a varied diet and you're going to save some money!

Make sure you try and feed your chickens with healthy foods such as rice, pasta, oats, fruit, vegetables, and wholemeal bread. As a general rule, if you can enjoy meat as much as they can. However, this excludes any fatty food or food with a lot of salt in it.

If we feed our girls scraps, we tend to cut them into little (thumbnail-sized) bits and chuck them straight to the floor in their cage. We're just putting the pellets in their trough.

You'd be amazed at some of the scraps that your chickens eat-pizza, spaghetti, and porridge, to name a few!

Before you feed your chickens' kitchen scraps, be sure to check your local regulations as in certain places (such as the UK). This can be surprisingly illegal.

5 Healthy Treats

Yeah, these chickens are probably spoiled! On top of their pellets and kitchen scraps, we're shocked that they still want to eat, but they do. Here are our top five healthy treats, which we occasionally spoil with:

Worms: they absolutely love worms.

Pumpkin: It contains a pumpkin plant.

Apple Cores: Simply drop the apple cores straight into the paper.

Broccoli: They can't get enough of it for some reason!

Porridge: They're just having this in the winter months though.

What you Shouldn't Feed Them

We've covered a lot of food throughout the post that you shouldn't feed chickens, so we're not going to repeat them again.

Certain foods that should not be fed to chickens include: avocado, rhubarb, garlic, chocolate, and any heavily processed meat (i.e., crisps).

Just remember, as a general rule, if you can eat chickens like that.

What Can Happen if Their Diet Isn't Right?

A great email we received from a reader last week was, how can I tell if my chicken's diet isn't right?'

The first thing to say was, should you note a significant change in their eating habits, make sure to have a vet look at them as soon as possible. And, if their food isn't perfect, there will be signs like that.

Egg production: If the season hasn't changed or their egg production drops drastically, this could mean that something is wrong in their diet.

General discontent and feather-picking: again, if the season hasn't shifted and they grab their feathers or each other's, this might mean that their diet isn't wrong.

Abnormal eggs: if you find that the eggs they lay are too small or consistently contain double yolks, this would indicate that their diet is not correct.

If you're searching for a helpful cheat sheet, be sure to check out what was developed by the Australian Government's Agricultural Department.

TOP 13 BEST EGG LAYING CHICKEN BREEDS

The Food and Agriculture Organization of the United Nations (FAO) has reported that in 2015 the cost of world egg production was USD 55 billion, and egg production was USD 70.4 million.

Before the Second World War, the largest egg production was obtained from small farms with around 400 chickens, but today, in large American egg-producing countries, chicken farms have reached 100,000 and even 1 million chickens in some cases. Nevertheless, given that the market for eggs raised in smaller chicken farms has increased, due to concerns about health and safety conditions in larger farms, the egg-producing sector has become very attractive to small enterprises.

Chickens are typically bred for meat or eggs, and each chicken farm must decide its business intent raising eggs, growing chickens for the meat industry, and providing a mixed farm, with both eggs laid chickens and chickens more appropriate for meat processing. As far as the most competitive egg-laying chickens are concerned, these are the best chicken breeds for this reason.

1. Australorp chicken breed

This breed, which originated in Australia, was produced in 1920, with deep roots in the Orpington breed. The name of this breed was given to the Orpington breed "Austral Orpington Club."

It's a chicken breed specialized in egg production, considered a true champion, as one hen of this type laid 364 eggs in 365 days. The Australorp breed is found in three color varieties: red, white, and black.

Australorp chickens are very healthy, with a rapid growth speed, beginning to lay eggs in the 5th month. They are ideal for growing in an enclosed environment but provide better egg production if they can walk freely in the open space. Such chickens are not good at flying, making it possible to expand in an open space, not having a large shelter. The hens of this breed are quite resilient, quickly going through cold winters, without impacting their egg-laying speed.

2. Lohmann Brown Classic chicken breed

It is the most common breed of laying chicken in the world and is used in almost every part of the world.

The Lohmann breed has a small size, with a bodyweight not exceeding 2 kilograms. A chicken of this breed produces up to 313 eggs per year, with a low feed consumption of just 110 grams per day.

3. Rhode Island Red chicken breed

The breed originated in the USA, where it is used for a dual purpose, both for eggs and meat. Such chickens are most common with small chicken farmers because they can easily adapt to backyard environments, have a high resistance to disease, and typically have a rather rough temperament. Rhode Island Red chicken can lay up to 260 eggs a year.

4. Sussex chicken breeds Similar to Rhode Island Red

This is a dual-purpose breed, which means that chickens are grown for eggs or meat. The breed has eight different colors, but the most famous are white chickens with black neck and tail feathers. Sussex chickens are very calm and tame, suitable for growing even in the yard. Chickens are capable of producing up to 250 eggs per year.

5. Golden Comet chicken breed

This breed is actually a widespread hybrid, known for its ability to produce between 250 and 300 eggs per year. The Golden Comets are very quiet and relaxed birds, ideal for open spaces and easy-going with other farm animals. The eggs have a brown shell on them.

6. Leghorn chicken breed

The breed originates in the port of Livorno, Italy, from a very old Italian community. It has 12 color variations, but the white chickens typically have the most feathers. Leghorn chickens have an average annual production of approximately 200 eggs, but up to 280 eggs may be produced. The eggs are 55-67 grams in weight and have a white shell. The brooding instinct is manifested very poorly, with the hens of this race brooding only in the proportion of 1-4 percent.

7. Marans chicken breed

It's a chicken breed native to France, with a very rich and colorful plumage. It has an annual production of 180-220 eggs and can be produced for both meat and eggs. The average egg is 60 grams, and the shell is brown.

8. Plymouth Rock chicken breed

This chicken breed is excellent for those who do not have a lot of experience growing chickens because they can easily adapt to a free-range lifestyle. These chickens are usually very tame and lay around 200 eggs a year, small to medium in size and brown in color. They can lay up to 280 eggs per year with proper care. The Plymouth Rock chickens are gray with white stripes.

9. Barnevelder chicken breed

This chicken breed is an unusual hybrid between the Asian jungle birds and the Dutch Landrace. Originally developed in Holland, it is known for its glossy feathers. The chickens lay up to 200 eggs a year, with a light brown speckled appearance and a small to medium size.

10. Buff Orpington chicken breed

Originally from Kent, England, this is the most popular variation of the Orpington breed and is ideal for backyard breeding because it is very tame and eager to socialize. Chickens prefer to get broody during the summer months, which is why they lay about 180 eggs each year.

11. Ameraucana chicken breed

This breed originated in South America and was named after the Araucanian Indians in Chile. It is also known by the name of Araucana. The Ameraucana breed developed as a hybrid between several hens and wild birds, from which they inherited the character that gives them the title of chickens that lay the healthiest eggs. The color of the eggshell has a blue-green shade; therefore, sometimes, it is also called "Easter eggs." It has an annual production of 170-180 eggs, weighing 53-60 grams. The egg production levels may not be important, but due to the low cholesterol content of the eggs, they are usually sold at a higher price.

12. La Bresse chicken breed

It is one of the oldest breeds of French chicken, created by a selection of local chicken populations. It has three color varieties: black, white, and gray, the most common being white.

A chicken produces 160-180 eggs per year, with a weight of 65-70 grams and a white shell. La Bresse is not only a good breeding chicken; it also has very tasty meat.

WHAT TIME DO HENS USUALLY LAY?

Raising chickens in the backyard is a fun and rewarding undertaking. Laying hens, bred for egg production, are plucky pets that reward your tender care with a steady supply of fresh and healthy food. Hens lay eggs during the day, most often in the night. The timing of oviposition or egg-laying varies with the breed of chicken and how much light exposure it gets.

Light exposure

The reproductive cycle of hens is controlled by photoperiod or light exposure. Hens need a minimum of 14 hours of light per day to lay eggs. They produce eggs at a maximum rate of 16 hours of light exposure. For particular, hens lay eggs within six hours of sunrise, or six hours of artificial light penetration for hens kept indoors. Hens with no access to artificial lighting in the hen-house should stop laying eggs in late fall for about two months. We start to lay down again as the days go on.

How the egg is made

Oviposition, or egg-laying, begins with ovulation. Hen ovulates by releasing an ovum, or egg yolk, from its ovary. Slowly, it travels down the hen's long oviduct, where the egg white, the shell layer, and the egg white form around the yolk. She lays the egg out of her cloaca, a common opening for her digestive, urinary, and intestinal tract. It takes about 26 hours, from ovulation to ovation.

Ovulation time

Hens usually ovulate in the evening but can ovulate as late as 3 p.m. The ovulation occurs about an hour after the egg has been laid. If a hen lays an egg in the morning, the egg may be postponed until the next day. The egg is going to be laid about 26 hours later. This is why hens regularly miss an egg-laying day.

Time of laying

A laying hen can at most only produce one egg every 28 hours. It does not ovulate and lay eggs in the dark, and the rate of egg production varies with the length and duration of the photoperiod. All these factors have an impact on the time of the day the egg is laid so that it varies with each egg. But it usually happens in the evening or in the early afternoon.

Genetic Factors

The hen's mating effects when the egg is laid. Brown-egg breeds tend to lie early in the day, while white-and tinted-egg breeds prefer to lie later in the day. Broiler hens, raised for meat production, lay eggs less often than laying hens. Broiler hens are allowed to lay their eggs before dawn.

HOW COLD IS TOO COLD FOR BACKYARD CHICKENS

How hot is it for chickens in the backyard? Below freezing, below zero, when it's too warm for me, there are all the responses I've learned. New chicken owners spending their first winter of chickens in a backyard coop may be worried about the actual winter weather. I live in a fairly mild region where the winter is typically not too extreme. We do get some winters that are colder than normal, and this often raises questions about how to keep the chickens happy and healthy. During the winter, I'm not too worried about my healthy flock members. Chickens are much cooler than heat tolerant. Indeed, changes in weather can have an effect on the flock. But if they're safe and well cared for, you shouldn't have chickens starving from the cold.

Signs of Cold Weather Stress

A chicken that feels stressed out of the cold is going to look cold. It might be huddled, not running around a bit. The feathers may be fluffed up considerably, and the chicken may sit on one foot, having the other tucked up in the feathers of the belly for warmth. This is the time to take action. Chickens are designed to self-regulate body temperature with their downy undercoat and increase food intake during cold weather. But there's a stage where they're going to need shelter even during the day. Heavy snow, rain, and below-freezing temperatures will need a few improvements to keep the flock healthy and happy. Don't wait too long, wondering how cold the chickens are.

A Well Designed Coop

A coop built for weather patterns in your area is the most important step you can take to plan for keeping chickens in cold weather. The coop can be heated before building, or the insulation can be applied afterward. Wrapping the coop in Tyvek's home wrap, or even attaching the tarps to the outside to break the wind, will help. The trick is to keep the wind cold and the rain out of the coop but to allow the water vapor to ventilate. Ventilation is so important to me. Don't keep the coop air-tight. Allowing good ventilation while still having warmth is crucial and will keep the chickens' warm while in the coop during extremely cold weather.

Holding the inside clean also avoids frostbites on combs, wattles, and feet. Applying a salve such as Waxlene to the combs and wattles will keep the frostbite from forming. Ammonia build-up will also be managed by keeping the coop clean. Clean up any drops easily. Imagine being in the coop during an ammonia smell outbreak! Not very friendly to any human person.

Should You Insulate the Coop?

A good coop structure will provide shelter from the wind, wet weather, and drafts. Isolation can be applied to the inside or outside of the coop. Hay balls are often used for insulation and can be stacked against the walls inside or outside the coop. Pay special attention to the north and west sides of the building.

Building insulation can also be applied during the coop construction process. Building a double-layer wall that traps air between the layers is one method. One is the use of traditional plywood-covered insulation to prevent chickens from pecking while filled.

I'm not in favor of adding mechanical heating equipment and heat lamps to the coop. Keep in mind that there are risks associated with the use of a heat lamp in a straw-filled system. When you plan on doing so, keep the 18 lamps away from any flammable material. Don't hang the lamp on the cord, and check the lamp frequently. I hesitate to discuss it because every year, a lot of farm families lose their whole flock and coop to a fire started by hanging a heat lamp in the coop. We have a regular bulb in our coop as a convenience to count chickens before we lock it up at night.

What About Sick or Injured Chickens and the Cold Weather?

It could be the best idea to move the vulnerable members of the flock to a cooler location for the duration of a cold snap. Weakened birds need TLC to maintain their strength and begin to heal. Using a crate in the laundry area and garage could be cooler to stop the chicken from using so much energy to keep it hot. During a cold snap, I brought a sick bird home to keep an eye on it. I'm sure many others have done the same thing. When you transfer the chicken back to the coop, once it's all right, do it on a warmer day. Being acclimated to rising conditions will be better if the day is colder.

Keeping the Drinking Water from Freezing

This is a matter for many of us in the winter. If you're not home enough to bring thawed water to the flock during the day, they won't be able to drink it when the water freezes. There are a few tricks that you can learn to use.

Using a small utility bucket, fill at least halfway with straw and sawdust. This will act as an insulating barrier and keep the water from freezing for a longer time. The air is also filtered by placing the bucket or rubber feed tub in the old tire.

Use a warmed dog water bowl during the day if power is available near the coop. Take it out and unplug at night so that the tank can be quickly refilled in the morning. For outdoor water containers, putting ping pong balls in the water helps the breeze keep the water from freezing. The movement of the ping pong balls will prevent the formation of the ice.

How Cold is Too Cold for Backyard Chickens?

It's hard to know exactly how cold the chickens in the backyard are. I believe it has a lot to do with the combination of proper housing and the overall health and fitness of your flock. There are people who raise chickens in extreme cold, without using artificial power. I'm surprised at the amount of warmth inside the coop on cold days, just because the chickens are inside.

For those of you who have harsh winter weather to months at a time, try these simple methods to keep your flock healthy and happy. Be alert and watch the flock members closely, search for frostbite or symptoms of cold weather pressure.

THE MOST RARE CHICKEN BREEDS

As we try to make our way of life greener, we look to try and buy more organic vegetables, we've switched from plastic straws to cardboard ones. A lot of people look at having backyard chickens as a way to make their own eggs, maybe food or natural fertilizer. That, in effect, makes it possible to cultivate an organic garden and so on.

But when we try to save our world, we should also look at what we can do for the wonderful animals that are dying out. We may not be able to raise a black panther, but we might try to save a few heritages and endangered/rare chicken breeds!

Dong Tao

The Dong Tao chicken breed is very rare and more so. They're a breed that's very popular for its meat in Vietnam. Originally from the village of Dong Tao in the Khoai Chau district of Vietnam, these chickens are also referred to as Dragon Chicken. The males can get around 13.5 lbs. And the females are around 9.9 lbs.

We are called Dragon Chickens because of their extremely thick bodies and large feet. The arms could be about the size of the adult male's hands. Because they've got very big legs and feet, they're not very good with their own nests, not that a lot of hens lie down. We were cheating around 2 or 3 a week, and most of them were split because of the chicken's shaky big legs.

Breeders need to be quite vigilant in finding the eggs and getting them into the incubators so that they have a better chance of getting the hatchlings

Ayam Cemani

If you think the Dong Tao is expensive, wait until you see the cost for the AyamCemani chicken breed. They say these are the Lamborghini of chickens, they are rare, beautiful, mysterious, and they were actually considered a sacred bird in Java, where they originated.

Such perfectly inked black chickens have black wings, wattles, ears, comb, beak, and feet. They hold on to themselves in such a way that a person can actually become quite mesmerized by this truly unique bird.

Another very special thing about this chicken breed is that it's not just its outer appearance that's completely black! The body, the liver, its hair, and even its bones are gray. The only thing that isn't black (though it's really dark) is its water. It was also a very common bird for various rituals.

Now, this breed is very rare, and if you can get them, there is usually a waiting list for them up to a year in advance. They can also get a price of $2,500 each, which is $5,000 for a pair of them!

AyamCemani is a mythical bird from Indonesia that has been connected with many mysterious, healing, and lucky charm legends over the years.

If you see this truly gorgeous hen, you can understand why. AyamCemani stands proudly upright, wearing her beautiful, soft, glossy black feathers that shine in the sun with a beetle of green and purple. This is a truly unique bird, in that not only are its feathers black, but comb, wattles, earlobes, ears, skin, ribs, and even organs black. While their blood is the natural color, it is also very dark and has been used for religious, sacrificial and ritual purposes throughout the ages in Indonesia.

Because of this, the bird has been used for many ceremonial rituals and is held in the highest respects. It is one of the rarest breeds, with most breeders usually sold out for up to a year in advance. Not only is it rare, but it is also one of the most expensive breeds, which is why it is known as the Lamborghini of poultry.

In many areas in Indonesia, these birds are highly valued, as they are considered holy animals. They're supposed to bring luck to those who keep them, and there's a belief that eating their meat can cure certain diseases.

Being such a rare bird, it doesn't bode well for their numbers that they're very common for various rituals.

History

AyamCemani is from Jakarta, Indonesia. We were thought to have been born from the Kedu, which is believed to have originated from the AyamBekisar, this breed of chicken hails from a group of islands in Indonesia. The origins of the AyamBekisar are believed to be the combination of domesticated red jungle birds with green jungle birds.

In the past, and still today, this breed is used as a foghorn by some seafarers on their boats because of the very distinct and unusual breeds of the crow.

The name of the Ayam part of the chicken breed means chicken in Indonesian. Cemani can mean either solid black in Sanskrit or Cemani village in the local Indonesian dialect.

These birds have been used as a symbol of community standing and wealth status. They're not the common people's chicken.

AyamCemani is not a chicken breed that you can easily find in any nearby poultry and ranch. You will need to order them from a licensed registered breeder with a strong bloodline stock. You will locate such breeders through the AyamCemani Breeders Association or on farms such as Greenfire Farms or Feathers Lovers Farms.

Check with your local animal welfare and shelter for more information on how to take the rescue, Plymouth Rock. They will also be able to help with any special needs, attention, or care they may need.

GENERAL

AyamCemani is an extremely rare exotic beauty with mystical qualities, the entrance of a person, and the personality that delights you. If you're hunting for the chicken that's going to be the star of your flock, that's the chicken for you. Although, you're likely going to have to wait up to a year to collect your bird(s). You can get them at certain lower end poultry vendors, but the quality and breeding requirements of these beauties will not be the same.

GROOMING

Make sure to de-worm your beautiful beauties on a regular basis, particularly if they are free-moving around the yard, playing with other domestic animals, and engaging with children. A good dust bath or two put under a comfortable shade tree or canopy with a touch of sage or lavender mixed in will be greatly enjoyed by these ladies. I love taking a dust bath to rid their beautiful feathers of insects and waste oils. A regular weekly or biweekly check for mites, lice, and various other parasites should be done to ensure a healthy flock.

DIET OR NUTRITION

These chickens are part of the occasional table scraps or consume most of the remaining vegetables or fruit as a tasty treat. As with other chickens, chicken pellets, grains, chicken mash or grain mixtures from 8 weeks of age and older are eaten. It's always best to feed your chickens their regular food first thing in the morning before they're allowed to forage.

The best thing for baby chickens is Chick Starter when they're under eight weeks old.

Laying hens should have extra protein and calcium in their diets to ensure the quality of their eggs to keep them in tip-top shape.

Please see our comprehensive guide to "Feeding your chickens" for more information on the different types of chicken feed for chicks, hens, laying hens, roosters, etc. and where to buy food and approximate feed costs.

SOCIALIZING THE BIRD

AyamCemani is mostly respectful of other breeds and their own animals. They have a calm nature, and they're going to settle in with just about any other breed. We make excellent mothers and brood chickens to feed other chicken eggs.

Always check how well the breed is going to get on with your current flock before you buy it, as you don't want to upset your coop or stress your current flock.

As with any newcomer to the roost, you will have to quarantine the bird for 7 –31 days to ensure that there are no unwanted critters or diseases that could spread to your current flock.

Onagadori

The Onagadori is a large bird that originates in Japan, where its name is loosely translated as "honorable bird." This breed was designated as a National Treasure in Japan in 1952, and to date, there are only about 250 birds left in Japan. These are exceptionally beautiful birds in which the tails of the roosters grow from a distance of 1.5 meters. One of the longest tails of This species recorded was 12 meters long. They've got about eighteen feathers in their tails that don't molt.

Their saddle hackles have also been known to be quite long and tend to grow quite fast. These come in three different color variants, black-brown yellow, black-brown gray, and green. The white range is my pick!

We need a considerable amount of attention and attention to their feathers. Most of the owners will keep them poised so that their feathers do not fall on the ground and cover their tails with silk ribbon to keep them in perfect condition.

Such magnificent ornamental chickens are raised as display birds and have been declared a Special Natural Monument in Kochi, Japan, where they originate.

He word Onagadori means eight "Long-tailed chickens" or "Honorable Fowls" in Japanese, who have had great pains in their breeding over the years.

The roosters have exceptionally long tail feathers, which do not molt so that they can grow too long for the whole life of the rooster. The minimum requirement of which their tails must be at least 2 meters long if they are to be considered a Longtail fowl.

The remainder of the feathers of the rooster, which cover the breast, the back, and the neck, usually molten like the feathers of the hens.

The Onagadori tail feathers have been recorded to be up to 27

There are other species, such as the Phoenix, which is a descendant of the Onagadori, which also have long tail feathers, but typically do not reach nearly 2 meters, and their tail feathers are liquid.

These beautiful birds require special housing, perches, and their tail feathers need extra care to be kept in top condition. Sometimes their tails are rolled up and secured with silk ties for protection, as the breeders take great pain not to allow the tail feathers to be dragged to the ground or to be roughed up, but to the wind and other elements.

HISTORY

The Onagadori is one of Japan's treasured monuments which, once declared as such, prohibited the export of eggs from the breeds. Therefore, every Onagadori seen these days outside Japan comes from eggs that landed in those countries before the bird was declared a Natural Japanese Monument.

It is because of this prohibition that these birds have been put as important on most preservation lists.

The roots of the Onagadori breed are quite ancient, and its ancestry is believed to have been a mixture of the green male jungle fowl and the red female jungle fowl. Such dogs were called Bekisar and originated from the Isle of Java.

Such jungle-birds were well known for their lovely long tails and crowns.

The hybrid of these two chickens was used to start a new breed of chicken, of which by 206 BC, there were many male birds with a long flowing tail.

These birds brought good money to Japan to export to China. Another breed came from these long-tailed chickens that were exported to China and called the Shokoku.

Approximately 700 to 900 AD, it was from the Shokoku chickens which Japan introduced from China that Japan bred another species called Totenko. The Totenko was brought up in Kochi and recorded by Professor Hiraoka.

It was from the crossbreeding of Totenko and Shokoku that the Onagadori was born, and the genus was improved from around 1912 to 1926 (Taiho period) to what we know today.

In the 1920s, to protect their lovely ears, they came to be bred as cage birds.

The first Onagadoris to arrive in Europe in the mid-1940s were known because Yokahama's as they left the port of Yokohama in Japan. These birds were not very adaptable to the European environment, prompting breeders to breed them with native, stronger breeds that shared the genes of Onagadori. As a result, a more robust Onagadori breed has come to be.

There are a few Onagadori in the USA, but they are very rare to come by, and they are often mistaken for the Phoenix Longtail.

Polverara

The Ploverara chicken breed is a very new one, others say, an antique breed that comes from Italy. They are a medium-sized crested chicken with a V-shaped red comb, small wattles, and white ear-lobes. They also have a beard that, together with their unique shaped crests, makes them look like little-bearded chefs. They come in two color variations, white and black. The white variant is pure white, and the black variety is the dark pigment that reflects a red beetle in the light.

Such chickens make incredible birds of prey. They lay a decent amount of medium to large white eggs. About 150 per year and their meat are little darker than most other chickens, but it is known for its delicious taste. The sad thing is that this exquisite chicken breed has almost all but vanished!

Ixworth

The Ixworth chicken breed was developed in Ixworth, Sussex, UK, and is becoming increasingly rare every year. This is sad because this dual-purpose chicken breed is an all-around, cheerful man and a great addition to any flock. It only comes in pure white and will lay between 160 and 220 cream / tinted eggs a year. Eggs are usually small to large in size. It was also a really good one after that for its very juicy, tasty meat. They're a large breed of chicken that's easy to handle, calm, and can be tamed.

Naked Neck

The Naked Neck has long been thought of as the "Turken" This is because it looks like a duck and a rabbit has been hit. However, there was once a story that this was the case. It is not a mutation that the chicken breed was designed to give the chicken up to 50% less feather protection than the normal chicken breed. Most of which are most visible on the chest where there are normally little to none. That's why these birds look like Turkey!

They come from Transylvania, which is why they are also known as Transylvanian Naked-Neck ducks. We have an outstanding quality of meat, which is very juicy, and are really good layers of large brown eggs. You can predict from between 200 to 250 eggs a year per hen.

Such chickens may look different, and at first sight, some people may even think there's something wrong with them. At first sight, you can see why people would think this way. The Naked-Neck chicken has up to fifty percent fewer feathers than other breeds, and a naked, plucked neck. That's why they're called Naked-Neck chickens or Transylvania Naked Neck chickens!

They may not look that pretty, but these birds are a very hardy breed that doesn't mind the weather, even with low feathers. They're going to need some nice warm shelter to warm up after a wintery walk around the garden. They can also withstand heat, but they will need some attention as they can get a sunburn, but there are easy preventive measures for this.

They're a big bird with a soft, friendly nature, and they can be quite amusing, as they're also quirky with their own amazing characters. They make great pets with a bonus of laying a decent number of medium-sized eggs for the table, and they are known as roasters for their good quality meat. They're actually quite a popular chicken in the backyard in France.

HISTORY

The Naked Neck chicken is believed to have originated in Transylvania. However, the breed as we know it today was mainly developed in Germany. The Naked Neck chicken was developed as a smooth-skinned dress bird that was much faster and easier to pluck.

The Naked Neck chicken was once believed to have been a hybrid cross between domestic turkey and chicken. As a result, the breed was often referred to as Turken. While the Naked-Neck chicken really looks like half a turkey and half a chicken. Scientist has long since proved that the two species are genetically incompatible. The bare neck trait in a chicken is caused by an "incompletely dominant allele." The Naked Neck gene has been shown to improve the size of the chicken breast and reduce the heat stress in some chicken breeds. If the gene is bred into different broiler breeds, it can help lower the chicken's body temperature to help with better body weight gain.

The Naked Neck chicken has proven to be an excellent forger and is also immune to most diseases.

They have been and still are a very popular bird in Europe, particularly in France and Germany.

However, they are not very popular in America, with very few breeders and backyard farms holding them. This is a pity because these chickens are very easy to tame, friendly and very calm. They were first seen in America around 1924 and were accepted into the Perfection Standard by the American Poultry Association in 1965.

Golden Campine

The numbers of the Golden Campines are in decline as they are usually overlooked in the case of breeds that are tougher to the climate, mature faster, and lay more eggs. But these smart, successful, and responsive birds need help to ensure that their numbers rise again. Just because they do not grow as quickly or almost as much as commercial/hybrid breeds does not mean that they are not useful. Hens lay about 180 to 200 medium white eggs a year, and if you kill chickens before 18 months, they make a nice bird of food. Not too big, but they're going to give a decent meal.

The breed is also unique in that the males are what is considered "hen feathered," which means that both males and females share healthy colors and patterns.

They're often considered to be an old breed that had spanned back to the time of Julius Caesar, who was believed to have owned a handful. To be more precise, he took a few to Belgium after a looting spree.

The Campine is a rare, uniquely beautiful chicken with a very upright stance, with tightly knit feathers that make them look larger than they are.

Such birds are great fliers, and they can be a bit sketchy and driving. They are very inquisitive birds, and although they don't like to be treated badly, they are very friendly. They're going to follow a human around the garden and talk back. They're not what's called a sitter, and they're very rarely going to crumble, so if you're trying to breed Campines, you might need a bridal hen to sit on their eggs.

Such busy chickens take quite a bit of space to roam around and forage about.

Where To Find These Birds To Add To Your Flock
Campine is a very rare bird on the vital conservation list, so it is best to find a certified breeder by organizations such as the Livestock Conservancy, the American Poultry Association, and the Society for the Conservation of Poultry Antiquities. There is also a club in the UK called the Rare Poultry Society, which includes breeders from all over the world, a lot of useful information and advice about the Campine. Try and avoid purchasing this rare ancient breed from poultry shops and plantations, as there are not many Campines in America. Registered breeders will also be able to help with any special needs, attention, or

care they may need. If you're planning on breeding your chickens, you're going to want to make sure they're from a good bloodline.

CARING FOR THE BIRD(s)

This is a comprehensive guide to chicken ownership. It covers where to start by choosing your ideal flock, the coop that would best suit your garden, your bird, and you to buy and bring your bird(s) home.

GENERAL

An exceptionally rare beauty that will be the treasure and centerpiece of any flock with its unique plumage and coloring.

GROOMING

One or two well-positioned dust baths are going a long way to keeping Campines pest and oil-free. There are several supplements that can be added to the soil to ensure that their feathers stay perfectly good. This may be quite a challenge, as these chickens will skitter away from being picked up, but they will have to be inspected for mites, lice, and any other parasites at least once a week. Always get your birds de-wormed on a regular basis, especially if they are around other animals or interact with children.

DIET AND NUTRITION

Make sure you get your regular chicken pellets, grains, chicken mash or grain mixture from 8 weeks of age and older first thing in the morning. This must be fed to them before they go out to forage every day to ensure that they are well fed.

The best thing for baby chickens is Chick Starter when they're under eight weeks old.

Laying hens should have extra protein and calcium in their diets to ensure the quality of their eggs to keep them in tip-top shape.

Vegetable and fruit table scraps are always welcomed by these busy birds and can go a long way to get them to comply with their weekly pest control.

Feeding your chickens properly would give your organic garden a lot of nutritious fertilizer to help your vegetables and flowers develop.

Please see our comprehensive guide to "Feeding your chickens" for more information on the different types of chicken feed for chicks, hens, laying hens, roosters, etc. and where to buy food and approximate feed costs.

SOCIALIZING THE BIRD(s)

Campines tend to shy away from other breeds, and it takes a long time for them to trust newcomers. They may be a flying sketch bird, but they're not an overly aggressive chicken, so it's best to get chickens that have a calmer nature to mix with Campines. They're not at all bridal hens, so if breeding is intended, it might be wise to look into getting bridal hens to add to the flock.

Always check how well the breed is going to get on with your current flocks before you buying it, as you don't want to upset your coop or stress your current flock.

As with any newcomer to the roost, you will have to quarantine the bird for 7 –31 days to ensure that there are no unwanted critters or diseases that could spread to your current flock.

Vorwerk

The Vorwerk is a dual-purpose chicken breed with a slate gray skin color, a stunning plumage, and a wonderful personality! They're not quiet animals, so they want to know what's going on around them. They are great foragers, have great meat, and lay about 180 medium brown eggs a year. Originally from Germany, they were built by Oskar Vorwerk. Oskar wanted a chicken breed that was an all-around pleaser, One that could lay a decent amount of eggs, have a great quality of meat, and look good. The Vorwerk was developed by the Andalusian, Buff Orpington, Buff Sussex, and Lakenvelder breeds. A few of the traits of the breed look much like the Lakenvelder, and one variety is often mistaken for the Lakenvelder.

Modern Game

Early Game breeds are mostly kept as display or ornamental birds these days. A long-legged, straight-up stance is similar to the supermodels of the poultry exhibition runways. We even come in a variety of stunning plumage colors that gives them the advantage of most poultry displays. Unfortunately, this breed is not as common as it used to be, and their numbers are declining. These beautiful birds take some care of themselves, as they are not very cold hardy and tend to prefer the hottest climates. But they're friendly birds, and they're full of lovely antics.

Classic Game Chickens are display and ornamental birds that have been raised as stunning counterparts to their gamecock ancestry.

We are the perfect show chicken from their dubbed combs and wattles to their stunning, willow, and dark faces. They are a tall, slender chicken with long, clean legs, well-shaped toes, beautiful color, and erect postures that make them look like supermodels of chicken breeds.

Shells: These are very weak layers of shells.

We lay medium white eggs. They lay between 50 and 80 eggs per year. They lay throughout the year but are more likely to lay in warmer weather. They begin to lay eggs at 22 weeks old.

Meat: They've got white skin. They're not meat chickens Breeding: they're not too difficult to breed unless you're going to show them. If so first time/novice breeders should seek advice from more advanced registered breeders Hens do get broody They are not really good brood hens They will sit on their eggs They will raise their chicks making surprisingly good mothers They have been known to mother other chickens/breeds chicks Show Bird: They were bred to be a show bird their bodies, posture, and personality aesthetically. These are the supermodels of the Poultry Show Houses.

Pets: Modern Game is sweet and inquisitive, who are attached to their humans. Other: Although they will not lay a lot of eggs, they will grace your garden with their beauty and style. They're not scratching almost as much as other breeds, so your garden and lawn won't get too messy from them.

HISTORY

Modern Game hens were developed due to the prohibition of cockfighting in 1849. Owners of fighting cocks took to display their birds at poultry shows, creating a new use for their game chickens.

Over the years of displaying these game birds, the poultry expectations for them have taken on more form, and more attractive qualities have been found in these game birds so that birds can gain awards and win shows.

With the aim of obtaining these requirements and producing winning bird breeders, we have begun to develop what we know today as the Modern Game Chickens.

The breed was first referred to as the Exhibition Game in the late 1800s and was not nearly as tall as the modern-day Modern Game Chickens.

By the 1880s, there was a dispute that the chickens should not be as tall as they were, and that some of the breeds used the name of the Old English Match.

By 1910 the breed as we know it today was developed and named Modern Game. Their sleek, tight, feathered frames, long, elegant legs, and hard feathers were all priced. They had quickly become a very popular bird show, and the Modern Game Club had been set up in England.

During the First World War, their numbers declined rapidly, as they were not a very useful bird, and the money was tight, so their popularity dropped.

By the time of the Second World War, their numbers were so few that the breed was thought to have become extinct.

But fortunately, the breed had also made its way to America in the late 1800s, as well as to various European countries.

The breed was brought back to life in the 1960s by Paul Hohmann, a German Breeder, who managed to get some eggs from America.

The Bantam variety of the Modern Game was developed in the 1860s, and in the 1900s, the breed was developed into the variety available today. As they were much cheaper and less expensive to maintain than the large Modern Game variety, the number of Modern Game Bantam varieties did not decline during the First World War.

TAKING CARE OF YOUR CHICKEN FLOCK

Your birds will require quite a bit of your daily care and well-being.

Keep your bird(s) healthy.

Vaccinations

It is best to tell the manufacturer what birds have been vaccinated against or before you buy the chickens.

If your chickens are combined with other poultry and domestic animals, it is best to have them vaccinated for Marek's disease.

It is also advisable to check vaccinations for your bird(s) with your local vet, animal shelter, and or animal welfare society.

Prevention is always better than cure, so if you can stop an infection, it's best to do so, particularly if it's widespread in your community.

Chickens are also prone not to show that they're sick until it's too late. We must behave as normal as possible to avoid being bullied by the rest of the flock.

You can handle most of the vaccines yourself, but it's best to let a doctor or an animal husbandry specialist do it.

Make sure you keep the vaccines up-to-date.

De-worming

All animals kept domestically or on a farm should be dewormed at regular intervals, especially as these pests can spread at an alarmingly rapid rate to infect your flock.

Preventing / Treating worms: There are different methods to do this, but it's always best to check with your doctor for the right one for your flock.

We will also instruct you on how often how to prescribe the drug to them.

Over counter solutions: one of the easiest and most cost-effective ways, costing around $20, is a liquid wormer.

You put the amount you need in their drinking water about once a month.

Natural remedies: There are also more natural remedies that you can do throughout the month that will also help to get rid of any existing worms and even some other pests like sand mites and ticks.

You can try crushing some garlic with your food or giving the pumpkin seeds, and even Apple Cider vinegar is going to do the trick.

Severe cases: In severe cases, it is always best to take the animal to the vet and ensure that you get the proper treatment to treat the rest of your flock.

An outbreak of worms: if your flock is getting worms, it is best to ensure that any other animals around them are also dewormed.

Make sure the ground on which they walk, feed-in, etc. are also worm-free.

Surroundings: there are products that can sanitize the soil to ensure that the worms are killed.

Keeping the grass short will help the sun's rays to kill any remaining parasitic eggs that may still be in the grass.

There are chemicals such as Soubenol, Flubenvet, and other herbal treatments that can be obtained from your local vet or veterinary suppliers.

Symptoms of worms: It's not easy to tell if your bird(s) have worms, but in the early stages, they may leave to lay eggs in unusual places.

They may have diarrhea with some worms; you will be able to see them in the chicken's droppings

They may eat more

They may lose a lot of weight

And if they have a gapeworm, it will stretch their necks as if they are gasping for air

Severe infestations can be fatal to the bird(s)

Types of worms:

Tapeworm

This is not that severe, but it can happen and damage the bird(s) immune system when they bind themselves to the intestinal lining of birds. You will need to take them to the vet and decide if they have tapeworms and the best treatment for this.

Gapeworm

These nasty worms cling to the bird(s) trachea, and that's why they make the bird stretch out their necks and look like they're gasping for air. Such worms are more common in chickens as they can be picked up from hosts, including snails, slugs, and worms.

Round-Worm

TAKING CARE OF YOUR FLOCK

Your birds can take quite a bit of your daily care and well-being.

Keeping your bird(s) on safe Vaccinations When purchasing your ducks, it is best to tell the manufacturer what the birds have been vaccinated for.

If your chickens are combined with other poultry and domestic animals, it is best to have them vaccinated for Marek's disease.

It is also recommended to confirm vaccines for your bird(s) with your nearest vet, animal shelter, and or animal welfare society.

Prevention is always better than cure, so if you can avoid an infection, it's best to do so, particularly if it's widespread in your town.

Chickens are also likely not to reveal that they're ill until it's too late. We must behave as normal as possible to avoid being harassed by the rest of the flock.

You can handle most of the vaccines yourself, but it's best to let a vet or an animal husbandry specialist do it.

Make sure you keep the vaccines up-to-date.

De-worming All animals kept indoors or on a ranch should be dewormed at regular intervals, especially as these pests can spread at an alarmingly rapid rate to kill your flock.

Preventing / Treating worms: There are different methods to do this, but it's always best to check with your doctor for the right one for your flock.

We will also instruct you on how often to prescribe the drug to them.

Over counter solutions: one of the simplest and most cost-effective ways, running about $20, is a fluid wormer.

You put the amount you need in their drinking water about once a month.

Natural remedies: There are also more natural remedies that you can do throughout the month that will also help to get rid of any potential worms and even some other insects like sand mites and ticks.

You can try grinding the garlic with your meat and offering the pumpkin seeds, and even Apple Cider vinegar is going to do the trick.

Serious cases: In severe cases, it is always best to take the dog to the vet to ensure that you get the proper treatment to treat the rest of your family.

An epidemic of worms: if your flock has worms, it is best to ensure that any other animals around them are still dewormed.

Make sure the soil on which they run, eat on, etc. are also worm-free.

Surroundings: there are materials that can sanitize the soil and ensure that the worms are destroyed.

Holding the grass short will help the sun's rays consume any remaining insect eggs that may still be in the grass.

There are drugs such as Soubenol, Flubenvet, and other herbal remedies that can be purchased from your vet and pharmaceutical distributors.

Symptoms of worms: It's not easy to tell if your bird(s) has worms, but in the early stages, they can leave to lay eggs in unusual places.

They may have diarrhea—with some worms you will be able to see in the chickens falls, and they will feed more, they will lose a lot of weight And if they have gapeworm, they may extend their necks as if they were gasping for air Severe infestations can be deadly to the bird(s) Forms of worms: Tapeworm is not that widespread but can happen and will damage the bird(s) immune system when they strike.

Gapeworm Photo Source: extension.umaine.edu These disgusting worms are bound to the trachea bird(s), and that's why they make the bird stick out their necks and appear like they're gasping for air. Such worms are more common in chickens as they can be picked up from hosts, including snails, slugs, and worms.

Roundworm, there are a few types of these worms, the most common of which is the big roundworm. These can basically take place anywhere in the digestive system of the bird(s). You may be able to pick them up in your bird's drops.

Pest-free There are other forms of pests other than worms that can affect your flock.

These are quite normal and may happen even with the regular care of your coop/run. Fleas enjoy the warm weather and can be quite a nuisance in the summertime, particularly in the hottest climates.

Prevention / Treatment of fleas, mites, and lice: cleaning and treatment of coop, run, garden areas, and other domestic animals that may come into contact regularly is a must.

Check your birds often by inspecting their feathers close to their skin, particularly on their breasts, tails, and vents.

Several mites are going to get between the scaly areas of the chicken legs.

If they have one of these infections, they can be handled with different solutions depending on the parasite.

Over the counter solutions: you can get any supermarket or pet hospital over the counter treatments.

Please read and follow the guidelines if you are not certain that you will seek advice from your nearest vet or animal shelter.

Ensure that the areas in and around the coop or wherever the chicken's play has been cleaned.

Natural remedies: There are garlic sprays available, or a person can make their own by smashing 3x the whole cloves of garlic in 2 cups of water. You can also add a teaspoon of lavender, spearmint, thyme, berry, or cinnamon oil to the mixture.

Spray chickens, coop, walk, and a number of locations around the coop.

You can even add crushed garlic to their water or dry food.

Extreme cases: In severe cases, it is always best to take certain types of flea from the animal to stay near the eyes of the bird, and a serious infestation of these can lead to blindness. If the chicken is in severe discomfort, it is best to have the infestation treated by a vet.

An insect outbreak: When one bird has fleas, it is almost certain that the rest of your flock has fleas. Every bird must be handled, its coop fully washed, just like the surrounding areas.

Ensure that all the animals are handled as well.

Once you've washed the coop, make sure you take off any socks, boots, etc. before you get back. These should be washed and cleaned up afterward, as you don't want to catch them in your house.

The surroundings:: make sure you keep the grass low as these insects appear to grow in the lawn.

There are both chemical and natural treatments in the garden to get rid of the pests.

Symptoms of pests such as mites, fleas, and lice, these three pests tend to show the same signs of infestation. Your birds will show the following most common symptoms that may be irritated by these parasites: discomfort and blood loss Decrease egg production Continuous scratching Irritability General malaise Restlessness See feathers deteriorate in patches and have raw skin spots Some infestations may cause blindness and even death. The pests that you may encounter with your bird(s) are:

Mites:

Such scary little red critters are distantly related to no-other than a spider.

They do come in three varieties:

Northern Fowl Mite: they love to live in the Coop's vent area, but they are quite happy to live on chicken as well.

Red Mite: these are the most annoying mites, and once an infestation happens, it's really hard to get rid of them. You may even need to get a qualified pest control to get rid of them. We love to live in nest boxes and other coop nooks and crannies. They're going to feed on chicken's blood during the night.

Scaly-leg Mite: these horrid little critters live in the scaly areas of the chicken leg. This can make the bird go lame if it's not handled on time. They're going to make the chicken leg thick, rough and swollen.

Lice:

Such pesky critters suck on the feathers of the chicken and the flakes of the hair. They are very annoying to the chicken, and they lay their eggs at the base of the feathers. Several situations are so serious that the bird is unable to collect the eggs.

There are about 50 different kinds of lice that can be found on chickens. Ask your local poultry specialist for more in-depth information on these.

Fleas

Most of the chicken fleas you can see are only about 5% of what is actually on the bird. The remaining 95% or the flea species is either larvae or egg-shaped on the animal.

Fleas can survive in a long grass for a short time, but they need a host to survive. They live on a bird and tend to breed rather quickly as soon as they are well fed.

Consider sprinkling FGDE on the coop wall, nesting boxes, roosting areas, and it can also be dusted on your flock (always check the directions before applying it).

While garlic is excellent as a general deterrent to most pests and worms, there is a risk of Heinz Anemia. This is because garlic is part of the family of onions. Onion is not a recommended source of food for your birds.

Apple Cider Vinegar sprinkled gently on your flock feathers as well as some herbs like mint will keep them away.

Ticks

Poultry ticks are sly critters that you may not notice on the bird. That's because they're hidden in the coop during the day to feed their host at night.

Such ticks are also borne by wild birds and are very common in nests such as vultures, buzzards, egrets, etc. They live in dark crevices between the wooden slats of the coop or in cracks in the floor.

They love the heat, the damp, and the humid air. Although the very cold weather is going to kill them, it's best to keep your coop tick-free no matter the season.

The creepy thing about poultry ticks is that they can survive without feeding for up to 4 years.

Effect on the flock: There are many serious diseases that these critters can inflict, including increasing paralysis of the foot, wing, and respiratory process. They can cause severe anemia, depression, and weight loss to the bird.

Signs and symptoms of chicken ticks: Agitated chickens at night, they can hurry and do not want to coop, they may become aggressive, and general malaise in the bird(s).

Increased egg production Treatment: There are alternative treatments that can be obtained at the local animal veterinarian or live poultry distributor.

If the chickens are housed in your local animal shelter, they will be able to help you with the cure.

Because ticks may have some nasty side effects if you've had a Poultry tick epidemic, it's best to get your flock /bird(s) checked over by the vet.

De-tick the coop Clear the birds from the coop.

It may be best practice to set up a clean, temporary home for a day or two.

Remove all the nesting boxes, the water, the food bowls, and, if you can, the roosting pots.

Use the cleaner that you purchased and clean the coop, nesting boxes, and roosting posts with it.

Use a high-pressure hose to blow out coops, nest boxes, and clean the roosting posts.

If there are holes between the frames, it may be safer to cover them with caulk once the coop has dried out.

If your nesting boxes are also made of wooden boards that have holes, caulk them, too.

Such ticks like to live and breed between sheets, knots in the wood, or small cracks or crevices they may locate.

Once the coop has been cleaned, you can let your birds go back to the coop.

Once you've had one infestation, it's best to always check it out every time you clean your coop.

Grooming Although most chickens do not require a lot of grooming, they still like to keep their feathers well trimmed and clean.

Show birds do require extra care and maintenance, even a bath! The daily gals can also be bathed periodically.

Bathing your chickens

Sometimes you may need to bathe your hen(s) like most other pets.

You're going to need a big bath to dip the bird in comfortably.

Fill the tub with warm water. You can put some soap sweaters in your bathtub, some baby shampoo or some mild soap.

Or you can gently apply the soap to your feathers.

Ensure that you hold her softly but firmly and that you don't worry too much about her.

Once you've soaped her, make sure you wash all the soap off her feathers.

Several people are going out and giving their hens a good dry blow with a hot to a cold hairdryer.

Clipping nails

Most of the chicken's nails are obviously damaged from their foraging and scratching. But there are some occasions or breeds that needed to be cut, or the nail gets too long, curls, and can cause a bird's health problems.

If you don't feel comfortable doing this, you can ask your local vet or live poultry supplier to help out.

If you're okay with that, you'll need a pet nail clipper.

Clip the nail, taking care as not to clip it too long or clip the pinkish part of the nail (quick) that will cause it to bleed and injure the bird.

Clipping wings

If you're worried about your birds flying in the coop and taking in your neighbor's yard, there's a chance to clip their wings.

This can be done by yourself (again, if you know how to do it and are comfortable with it).

It is best to first figure out how to do this or do it under observation, as you do not want to injure or permanently damage the wings of the bird.

Normally, just one wing clip allows the bird to become erratic when it tries to take off.

Each time the bird molts, you'll have to trim and slice the wing again as the feathers grow back

Dust baths

Chicken owners may find dirt patches that look like a chicken made a bit of a nest, but actually, it's more likely to be a dirt bath patch. The chicken is going to scratch a hole to loosen the dirt. They'll nest in and wiggle around, flapping out their wings and spewing up the dust. This is how they clean themselves up in a dust bath.

The dust bath helps to remove internal bacteria and extra oil from their feathers and hair, which helps to make them waterproof.

Dust bathing for chicken is just as normal human bathing is a way to groom and clean up.

The first time you encounter this, you might think that your chicken is in trouble because it's quite a sight to behold.

There are many ways to make a dirt bath for your chicken, and we have a few ideas for you in our "Chicken Dirt Baths" article. The article explains the forms of sand, nutrients, and the right dust baths for winter, etc. It is important to make sure they have some good loose sand to fluff around in the water, and you can also apply some peat moss to the heap.

Clean, warm, and comfortable in the cold and clean, hot, and new in the sun. The mean heart rate for chickens is usually 280 to 315 beats per minute.

Their average body temperature under normal conditions should be between 102 and 103 degrees Fahrenheit.

A hen will take about 30 to 35 breaths per minute, while a rooster will take about 18 to 20 breaths per minute on average.

The average lifespan for chickens depends on their laying habits and can range from 2 years to 20 years (this also depends on the chicken breed).

Because their bodies work differently from humans and other species, they seem to need some extra care at both the warm and colder periods of the year.

The hot summer months

OVERVIEW Now that you've decided whether keeping chickens is right for you, why, where, and how many chickens you can keep, the breed you want and age. It's time to look at what it takes to take care of your family.

Your birds should need quite a bit of your daily care and well-being.

TAKING CARE OF YOUR FLOCK: Your birds can take quite a bit of your daily care and well-being.

Keeping your bird(s) safe Vaccinations: When buying your ducks, it is best to tell the manufacturer what the birds have been vaccinated for.

If your chickens are combined with other poultry and domestic animals, it is best to have them vaccinated for Marek's disease.

It is also best to confirm vaccines for your bird(s) with your nearest vet, animal shelter, and or animal welfare society.

Prevention is always better than cure, so if you can stop an infection, it's best to do so, particularly if it's widespread in your community.

Chickens are also likely not to reveal that they're ill until it's too late. We must behave as normal as possible to avoid being harassed by the rest of the flock.

You can handle most of the vaccines yourself, but it's best to let a vet or an animal husbandry specialist do it.

Make sure you keep the vaccines up-to-date.

De-worming all animals kept indoors, or in a ranch, it should be dewormed at regular intervals, especially as these pests can spread at an alarmingly rapid rate to kill your flock.

Preventing / Treating worms: There are different methods to do this, but it's always best to check with your doctor for the right one for your flock.

We will also instruct you on how often to prescribe the drug to them.

Over counter solutions: One of the simplest and most cost-effective ways is running to about $20, it's a fluid wormer.

You put the amount you need in their drinking water about once a month.

Natural remedies: There are also more natural remedies that you can do throughout the month that will also help to get rid of any potential worms and even some other insects like sand mites and ticks.

You can try grinding the garlic with your meat and offering the pumpkin seeds, and even Apple Cider vinegar is going to do the trick.

Serious cases: In severe cases, it is always best to take the dog to the vet to ensure that you get the proper treatment to treat the rest of your family.

An epidemic of worms: if your flocks have worms, it is best to ensure that any other animals around them are still dewormed.

Make sure the soil on which they run, eat on, etc. is also worm-free.

Surroundings: there are materials that can sanitize the soil and ensure that the worms are destroyed.

Holding the grass short will help the sun's rays consume any remaining insect eggs that may still be in the grass.

There are drugs such as Soubenol, Flubenvet, and other herbal remedies that can be purchased from your vet and pharmaceutical distributors.

Symptoms of worms: It's not easy to tell if your bird(s) has worms, but in the early stages, they can leave to lay eggs in unusual places.

They may have diarrhea, with some worms, you will be able to see in the chicken's falls, they will feed more, they will lose a lot of weight, and if they have gapeworm, they may extend their necks as if they were gasping for air. Severe infestations can be deadly to the bird(s).

Forms of worms: Tapeworm is not that widespread but can happen and will damage the bird(s) immune system when they strike.

Gapeworm Photo Source: extension.umaine.edu. These disgusting worms are bound to the trachea bird(s), and that's why they make the bird stick out their necks and appear like they're gasping for air. Such worms are more common in chickens as they can be picked up from hosts, including snails, slugs, and worms.

Roundworm: There are a few varieties of these worms, the most common of which is the big roundworm. These can basically take place anywhere in the digestive system of the bird(s). You may be able to pick them up in your bird's drops.

There are other types of insects other than worms that can damage your flock.

These are quite normal and may happen even with the regular care of your coop/run. Fleas enjoy the warm weather and can be quite a nuisance in the summertime, particularly in the hottest climates.

Prevention / Care of fleas, mites, and lice: washing and care of coop, yard, garden areas, and other domestic animals that may come into contact periodically is a must.

Check your birds often by inspecting their feathers close to their skin, particularly on their breasts, tails, and vents.

Several mites are going to get between the scaly areas of the chicken legs.

If they have one of these infections, they can be handled with different solutions depending on the parasite.

Over the counter solutions: you can get any supermarket or pet hospital over the counter medications.

Please read and follow the guidelines, if you are not certain that you will seek advice from your nearest vet or animal shelter.

Ensure that the areas in and around the coop or wherever the chicken's play has been cleaned.

Natural remedies: There are garlic sprays available, or a person can make their own by smashing 3x whole cloves of garlic in 2 cups of water. You can also add a teaspoon of lavender, spearmint, thyme, berry, or cinnamon oil to the mixture.

Spray chickens, coop, farm, and a number of locations around the coop.

You can even apply crushed garlic to their water or dry food.

Extreme cases: In severe cases, it is always best to take certain types of flea from the animal to stay near the eyes of the bird, and a serious infestation of these can lead to blindness. If the chicken is in severe discomfort, it is safe to have the infestation handled by a vet.

An insect outbreak: When one bird has fleas, it is almost certain that the rest of your flock has fleas. Every bird must be handled, its coop fully washed, just like the surrounding areas.

Ensure that all the animals are handled as well.

Once you've washed the coop, make sure you take off any socks, boots, etc. before you get back. These should be washed and cleaned up afterward, as you don't want to catch them in your house.

The surroundings: make sure you keep the grass low as these insects appear to grow in the lawn.

There are both synthetic and organic methods in the greenhouse to get rid of the insects.

Symptoms of insects such as mites, fleas, and lice: All three species tend to show the same symptoms of infestation. Your birds should exhibit the following most common symptoms that may be aggravated by these parasites, pain and blood loss, Decrease egg production, Constant scratching, Irritability, General malaise, Restlessness, See feathers deteriorate in patches and have damaged skin spots. Many infestations can cause blindness and even death. The insects that you may find with your bird(s) are Mites.

They do come in three varieties:

Northern Fowl Mite: they love to live in the Coop's vent area, but they are quite happy to live on chicken as well.

Red Mite: these are the most annoying mites, and once an infestation happens, it's really hard to get rid of them. You may even need to get a qualified pest control to get rid of them. We love to live in nest boxes and other coop nooks and crannies. They're going to feed on chicken's blood during the day.

Scaly-leg Mite: these horrid little critters live in the scaly areas of the chicken leg. This can make the bird go lame if it's not handled on time. They're going to make the chicken leg thick, rough and swollen.

Lice: These nasty critters feed on chicken feathers and hair flakes. These are very irritating to the hen because these lay their eggs at the base of the feathers. Many situations are so serious that the bird is unable to collect the eggs.

There are some 50 different kinds of lice that can be present on poultry. Ask your local poultry specialist for more in-depth information on these.

Fleas Most of the chicken fleas you can see are only about 5 percent of what is currently on the bird. The remaining 95% or the flea species is either larvae or egg-shaped on the animal.

Fleas can live in a long grass for a short time, but they need a host to survive. They live on a bird and tend to breed rather quickly as soon as they are well fed.

Consider sprinkling FGDE on the coop wall, nesting boxes, roosting areas, and it can also be dusted on your flock (always check the directions before applying it).

While garlic is excellent as a general deterrent to most pests and worms, there is a risk of Heinz Anemia. This is because garlic is part of the family of onions. Onion is not a good source of food for your pets.

Apple Cider Vinegar sprinkled gently on your flock feathers as well as some herbs like mint will keep them away.

Ticks Poultry ticks are sly critters that you may not spot on the bird. That's because they're hidden in the coop during the day to feed their host at night.

Such ticks are, in addition, borne by wild birds and are very common in nests such as vultures, buzzards, egrets, etc. They live in dark crevices between the wooden slats of the coop or in cracks in the floor.

They love the heat, the damp, and the humid air. Although the really cold weather is going to kill them, it's best to keep your coop tick-free no matter the season.

The colder winter months

Most chicken breeds survive the winter without any complications, as their feather allows for great insulation. There are also some types of chickens that do not take too well in extremely cold climates, so it is best to check the breed and assess their temperature toughness.

Nevertheless, the cold can have a serious effect on even the toughest animal, particularly when they lie down for the night.

Look out for the following signs that your chickens are suffering from the cold weather.

Egg production decreases: The birds will huddle together in groups. There will be a rise in their appetites. They will not consume as much food. Your birds may have behavioral changes. They will not be able to ward off infection as well in the snow.

They may have problems with their feet if they are constantly walking around in the damp. Older birds will be more affected by the cold. Some birds may suffer from frostbite. Help prevent damage to your flock and keep them warm by adding energy-rich fats and oils to their diet (see your local vet for advice). This will also reduce the consumption of food for birds in the cold. Provides a good source of energy to help the bird keep warm. Make sure there is no excess of groundwater, as the birds may be tempted to drink, and that could lead to worms. It is particularly good to ensure a rigid de-worming routine in these cold months. Something that you need to discuss with your local vet.

Isolate their coop and keep it elevated from the ground, keeping the birds safe in the rain.

Heating lamps are a good option, but they also come with their dangers. It's always best to check these as they could be a fire hazard.

Keep a close eye on your birds for any winter malaise, so that you can deal with the situation early and avoid any future outbreaks or dire consequences for your bird(s).

Keep your flock clean, sanitized, and keep healthy.

Feeding meals and foraging feasts- There is a clear rule of thumb for feeding and handling the flock, and this is the 90/10 rule. This is to ensure that 90 percent of your chicken's average intake of food is their healthy feed, with 10 percent left for delicious treatments.

We have a minimum of 38 different nutrients at the right level. These are typically found in different "Full Feeds" for poultry.

Feed your chickens in the morning before they go to forage (every feed pack must come with instructions on how much to feed your chickens). This way, you're going to make sure you stick to the 90/10 percent rule. Chickens will have their normal nutrient requirements in their feed before they go out to peck and forage. Foraging foods are also considered to be part of their therapies.

Full feeds come with all the bird nutrients you'll need. A common mistake that people make is trying to replace these feeds.

It's better to give some form of the substitute as a medication instead, along with the medications, just make sure you're not over-supplementing your bird(s). It is best to talk to a vet, animal shelter, or a poultry farmer for any advice.

Feeding the chicks: chickens from day 1 to 18 weeks old Use a complete starter feed.

Do not give treatment until the first egg has been laid or the roosters are older than 18 weeks.

Laying hens: Laying hens need a total of 38 nutrients in their complete feed, of which they should have at least 0.25 (half cup) pounds of each day.

You can get a variety of Layer feeds for birds producing table eggs.

Broiler feeds for birds that contain hatching eggs.

Feed the chickens in the night. Use Complete feeds for adults and chicks as described above.

Scratch grains are more likely to be treated and should NOT be mixed with their regular food.

Ensure that you provide enough grit to the chicken to help digest any grain or food that might require it. You can get the stuffed grit that's chicken size, fine gravel, or rough soil.

Oyster shells are too small to make a good meal, and you need to be careful when feeding them. Chickens do not need too much calcium and may have an adverse effect if they overdose.

Foraging

Chickens love to forage and try new plants and little bits they can dig around the garden.

They're quite in tune with their brains, so they don't tend to eat what isn't healthy for them. But there are some chickens that are going to eat just about anything, so you can take care of the kind of flowers, herbs, berries, etc. that you may have in the greenhouse if you keep chickens.

You can throw a tablespoon or two of the scratch grains around where they feed and scratch during the day. It's best to do that in the afternoons.

What chickens can eat: The darker green leafy vegetables tend to produce a darker egg yolk.

A few healthy favorites include; perennial favorites, roses, ferns, coneflowers, daisies, hostesses, and daylilies.

Vegetable favorites; kale, Swiss chard, carrots, lettuce, beets, and broccoli.

Fruits Favorites: fruit should be seasoned Strawberries, blueberries, avocado meat, and watermelon Favorites: cilantro, thyme, basil, mint, oregano, parsley, and lavender. Then there are foods that contain toxins and substances that can make them sick or even cause death.

Avocado pits and skin contains a poison called persin, which is poisonous to chickens. No moldy or rotting feed and food containing a lot of salt, as this may be harmful to your flock.

No meat products Rhubarb with severe weather exposure typically contain a high concentration of oxalic acid that is poisonous to poultry. Rhubarb also produces anthraquinones that have a laxative effect on your birds.

Try to avoid beans of any kind, particularly undercooked ones, as they may contain something called hemagglutinin, which acts as a digestion inhibitor.

Onions are not only harmful to your birds, but they can give their eggs a strange taste as well.

Garlic may be provided in abundance to protect against certain insects, but keep in mind that it may have an effect on the flavor of the eggs.

Chicken friendly garden. If your birds are going to be free in your garden, it's best to take care that it's a chicken-friendly garden.

Keep in mind that it's like scraping the ground, foraging, and eating plants.

Any plants or areas you don't want them scratching inside, you might want to look at putting chicken proofing in the form of tunnels or chicken wires around them. Especially if you've got a vegetable patch or a herb patch.

Keep the crops as chicken safe as you can.

A good old chicken time and general maintenance.

Spending time with your flock every day: Chickens are really clever and quite sociable animals. Most of the breeds will flee when they see their humans entering the yard. We also like to lead you around thinking about their day.

As with any pet we want love, you can spend at least an hour or two with your herd.

Even if you're just walking through your garden with them trailing behind you, give them a word, or if they want a cuddle. Inspect their feathers for the critters to make sure they look after themselves.

They like to be chewed on the back of their necks—gently, though!

You could even play with them and show them tricks.

It's very important to develop a trusting relationship with your bird(s).

General cleaning: Every day, feed the birds each morning before they let them fly, giving them treats in the afternoon and early evening.

Save eggs (collecting them daily will prevent them from being eaten). Fresh food (make sure there are no falls or foreign objects in the bowl)

Fresh water (make sure you don't kill them).

It's a great idea to add some beautiful herbs to their bedding, such as lavender, lemon balm, and some fresh mint oil.

Give the birds a thorough check. To do this, gently pick up the hen and start working your way down to their feet with your head.

You need to test for weight loss, sores, fleas, mites, watery eyes, or the odd color of your combs. There should be no scab or hard-swollen vine. The hen's wind is usually moist and pink. The legs should be smooth, not scaly, and there should be no black spots. Their breast bones should not stand out that could suggest weight loss.

Once a month
Do a good thing to wash the coop.

Replace all the bedding and wash the nesting boxes thoroughly.

Wash all of the things in the coop, such as roosts, feeders, and water bowls.

Scrap any drop and completely clear out any stray, line the floors, etc.

Check ventilation and vents to ensure that the coop is adequately cleaned and correctly sealed.

Replace and replace any chicken wire that may be required, as well as various items such as nesting boxes, etc. in the coop.

Each six months

De-worm chickens Test vaccines Ensure that special summer and winter precautions are taken

Once a year

Remove all heavy equipment such as lights, fans, coops themselves, etc. if necessary.

If you can, have a vet check up on your flock to make sure they're healthy.

CONCLUSION

Raising a chicken flock at home can be a good experience and a source of fun. This talks about living beings and accountability as a family project. Home chicken flocks can also be an excellent source of low-cost, high-quality poultry products. This publication should provide the basic tools for starting a successful flock.

Andrew McDeere

BEEKEEPING

For beginners

A Complete guide to build your first hive, raise the bee colony and best to handle the honey production

Copyright © 2019 Publishing.

All Rights Reserved.

Author: Andrew McDeere

No part of this publication may be reproduced, distributed, or transmitted in any form or by any means, including photocopying, recording, or other electronic or mechanical methods, or by any information storage and retrieval system without the prior written permission of the publisher, except in the case of very brief quotations embodied in critical reviews and certain other noncommercial uses permitted by copyright law.

INTRODUCTION

Bees are insects which are strongly linked to wasps and ants, renowned for their position in pollination and, in the event of the best established bee species, western honey bee, for the production of honey and beeswax. Bees are a monophyletic group within the Apoidea superfamily and are currently regarded a clade called Anthophila. There are more than 16,000 known species of bees in seven recognized biological families. They are discovered on every continent except Antarctica, in every habitat on the planet that includes insect-pollinated flowering plants.

Some species, including honey bees, bulbs and stingless bees, live socially in colonies. Bees are adjusted for the production of nectar and pollen, the former mainly as an energy source and the latter mainly for proteins and other nutrients. Most pollen is used as larvae meat. Bee pollination is both ecologically and socially significant. The decrease in wild bees has improved the importance of pollination by commercially controlled honey bee hives.

Bees vary in quantity from small stingless bee species with a length of less than 2 millimeters (0.08 in) to Megachile pluto, the biggest leaf cutter bee population with a duration of 39 millimeters (1.54 in) for women. Halictidae or sweat bees are the most prevalent bees in the Northern Hemisphere, but they are tiny and often mistaken for wasps or insects. Vertebrate bee predators include birds such as bee-eaters; insect predators include bee-wolves and dragonflies.

Human apiculture or apiculture has been practiced for millennia, at least since ancient Egypt and ancient Greece. Besides honey and pollination, honey bees generate beeswax, royal jelly and propolis. Bees have emerged in mythology and folklore, throughout all stages of art and literature, from ancient times to the current, though mainly in the Northern Hemisphere, where apiculture is much more prevalent.

An assessment of 353 wild bee and hoverfly species across Britain from 1980 to 2013 discovered that insects were removed from a third of the sites they populated in 1980.

Honey bees, like all living things, vary in their traits across the species. Genetic differences across these breeds can lead to differences in attributes like temperament, disease resistance, productivity, color and much more. The environment has a huge impact on differences among bee colonies due to stimuli and response, but the genetic makeup of a colony is the basis for many of the characteristics that define a particular subspecies of honey bee. For as long as honey bees have been domesticated, beekeepers have known that different genetic stocks have distinctive differences that can be used to their advantage or ignored to their disadvantage. Whether it be pollination, a honey crop, bee reproduction, resiliency or otherwise, it is important to have a general grasp on what this means for you and your Beekeeping Goals.

WHAT IS BEE STOCK? A SUBSPECIES OF APIS MELLIFERA?

"Stock," as defined by David Tarpy at North Carolina State University, is a term to define a loose combination of traits that characterize a particular group of bees. Such groups can be divided by the species, race, region, population, or breeding line in a commercial operation. In many ways, the easiest way to understand Bee Stock is to compare it to the way we have followed and tracked the pedigree of racing horses throughout the ages. Often there are lines of heredity that go back hundreds of years in quality stock.

It is important to understand that although most of the honey bees for purchase come from these so-called races of honey bees, from what we know about honey bee reproduction and queen mating, the "purity" of the stock is not always easy to control. Beyond that, these races are still defined from the Old World. Dr. Al Dietz defined the terms "bee stock" and "races" as "The geographic races of bees are the results of natural selection in their homeland. That is, the bees became adjusted to their original environment, but not always to the economic requirements of beekeepers. Therefore, they are not the result, but the raw material for breeding." His statement (1992. Honey bees of the world. The Hive and the Honey Bee) helps us to understand that although these genetic strains are rooted in history, they are still just a way to help us classify basic differences and are not impervious to flaws.

THINGS TO CONSIDER WHEN DECIDING ON A BEE STOCK

There are 5 main points to consider when searching for and choosing a bee stock according to the American Bee Journal. Others take it to a a level of detail that may be beyond a new beekeeper or even a practiced beekeeper of 5 years. These types of selection criteria include:

Production

Location

Temperament

Disease resistance

Quality of products

Age of line

Reproduction Rates

Swarming Rates

Noted Range

Environmental Resilience

Much more

THE MAIN SUBSPECIES OF HONEY BEES (APIS MELLIFERA)

In the United States there are 6 main stocks of honey bees. Each strain has been studied and observed to have a variety of attributes that may be helpful to know in making your choice. Beyond that, there are local strains coming from different regions of the US and the world every year. It is always good practice to do research beyond these main strains to see if there is something that might be better suited for your area. This information comes from a variety of research institutions who have focused on making this a useful tool.

The Italian Honey Bee (Apis mellifera ligustica)

Italian Honey Bees are some of the most widely used races of honey bee stock. They originated in Italy, hence the name, and were brought to the United States in 1859. They are known for their prolific brood cycles and production, gentle nature and reluctance to swarm. As excellent producers, most commercial beekeepers will use Italians as their main source of production. They are very light colored, almost completely yellow in some colonies, making them aesthetically pleasing to the eye and fairly easy to identify.

Despite the well-rounded advantages of the Italian Bee, there are some drawbacks. They consume resources at a rapid pace due to their long brood cycles that can last deep into the fall.

They are notorious for robbing stores in weaker or neighboring hives.

Italian Bees tend to have more difficulty with natural pests and tend to have higher collapse rates because of this. The rationale as to why this happens is yet to be determined, but research is moving quickly due to their popularity.

Italian Honey Bees are great for almost any beekeeper due to their well-rounded nature and availability in packages and nucs.

The Russian Bee (from Primorsky Krai region of Russia)

Russian bees were brought to the United States in 1997 by the USDA in response to the increase in colony collapse due to parasites. They have been noted to have natural capabilities and colony tolerance to handle varroa and tracheal mites. In fact, the US Department of Agriculture's Honey Bee Breeding, Genetics and Physiology lab in Baton Rouge, Louisiana has shown results that many stocks of this breed contain half the mite load of standard commercial stocks.

Russian bees tend to rear brood only during times of nectar and pollen flows, making this subspecies heavily reliant on the surrounding environment. Also, less availability due to constraints on breeding make this bee significantly more difficult to obtain for hobbyists or "newbees."

Beyond these traits, Russian bees exhibit some unusual behaviors in comparison to other strains. For example, Russian honey bee colonies tend to contain a queen cell almost all the time, in comparison to most stocks, where a queen cell is only present during times of swarming or queen-replacement. Another interesting trait is that although Russian colonies tend to be more aggressive, research shows that when in the presence of other strains, there is significant cross-contamination of stock and an increased susceptibility to natural pests.

The Carniolan Bee (Apis mellifera carnica)

The Carniolan Bee is one of the top 2 most popular bee stocks in the United States. This strain is favored for a variety of reasons including:

Their explosive spring buildup makes it ideal for beekeepers looking to build up quickly before the summer

Carniolan Bees are extremely docile and take a lot of irritation to be agitated enough to sting.

Most notably, the Carniolan Bee has one of the longest tongues at 6.5 to 6.7 mm, which helps it pollinate crops like clover, meaning more sources of nutrition for the colony than other strains of honey bee stock.

Beyond these basic traits, due to the origin of this stock from central and Eastern Europe, these bees have been bred to be more tolerant of colder climates and rank among the best stocks for overwintering. These bees spend their winters in a tight cluster with a modest food supply and have proven to be a favorite for beekeepers in Slovenia, where beekeeping is of cultural significance.

Yet, there are some drawbacks with this strain, most notably, this bee stock tends to swarm more often than most other subspecies of bee. Some researchers attribute this to their explosive growth and comb production early in the year and even into times of dearth, as they do not require much food to survive in comparison to other bee strains.

Overall, this strain of honey bee is a great option for beekeepers who are concerned about shifting weather from warm to cold and damp or rougher winter seasons.

The Buckfast Bee (The mutt of honey bee stock)

The Buckfast Bee stock is named for the location of its hybridization and origin, Buckfast Abbey, in Devon in the United Kingdom. During the early 20th century, populations were being decimated by tracheal mites. Brother Adam (Karl Kehrle) who was in charge of beekeeping at the abbey, started to cross the strongest colonies who had survived in the area. The new stock of bees have become a favorite for those in similar environments as that of the British Isles.

The Buckfast bee shows strong resistance to some natural parasites.It has a strong knack for foraging and is not a strain that tends to swarm, making it more difficult to find these bees in the United States.Beyond this, there is often inbreeding with this strain over time. This decreases the characteristics such as resilient behavior against pests and other elements that make this aquality strain of honey bee.

The Caucasian Bee (Apis mellifera caucasica)

This bee stock was once very popular in the United States, but its lack of honey production overall has lessened its use among honey producers in the United States. Yet, there are still some commercial pollinators who use this strain due to its very long tongue; longer than Carniolan bee stock most of the time. Similar to the Carniolan bee, the Caucasian bee shares similar traits in temperament.

The lessened use of this strain in the US has increased its value among traditionalists because most stock is imported from Europe and then cross-bred with Carniolans (https://bees.wsu.edu/breeding-program/queens/). Even though the gradual build-up rate of the colony is slower than many largely used stocks, it allows for honey to be stored more efficiently near the brood. In other words, it doesn't proceed to a new comb until the previous one is completely filled.

For beekeepers who understand the importance of winter stores and the "heating blanket" in colder climates, this single trait could help your bees increase the chance of overwintering this year.

The German Bee (Apis mellifera mellifera)

The European Dark Bee, or German Dark Bee, was brought from Northern Eurasia in the colonial era. This subspecies has since then been segmented further into sub races of German Bees due to its hardiness. It is able to survive long, cold winters more often than other strains of honey bees. However, due to their defensive nature and susceptibility to brood diseases like American and European foulbrood, this stock has lost significant favor with beekeepers all over the world.

Although this strain of bee stock has lost significant value in the commercial sector, there are still researchers and hobbyists working hard to isolate the hardiness of this subspecies through tracking breeding values and data religiously.

For beekeepers in the US, this strain is most likely not available, and would not be a good choice unless you are familiar with natural diseases and parasites in the hive.

The Africanized Bee (The Misunderstood Bee)

The Africanized, or Killer Bee as most know it, is not even from Africa it originated in Brazil. This honey bee strain was a hybrid designed in a lab with the goal of increasing pest and parasite resistance, while at the same time increasing production. This bee stock showed great promise until 26 experimental swarms escaped quarantine and took over South America.

This highly aggressive strain of honey bee has some advantages, if one learns to work with them. They begin foraging at a younger age, typically produce more honey, and have a significantly smaller colony size, even though they reproduce at a faster pace. There are many stories of beekeepers working well with these bees for these positive traits.

BEGINNER BEEKEEPING: STEPS WITH A TOP BAR BEE HIVE

If you are just starting beekeeping or thinking about starting, then this is the time to catch the wave to get setup for bee season. The first year of caring for bees in the top bar hive is a simple setup.

You will need to:

1) Purchase or build a hive

2) Find a resource and order bees

3) Find a location for your hive

4) Purchase protective clothing

5) Coat the top bars with beeswax

6) Install the swarm or package of bees

7) General questions for setting up a hive

1) BUY OR BUILD A BEE HIVE

Purchase a fully assembled hive from top bar Beehives for Sale page, BackYardHive, or build your own from the Bee Hive Plans on our website. They offer fully assembled hives since many folks don't have the wood shop or the time to build their own hives.

If you build a hive from their plans, I highly suggest you purchase top bars as the top bars are the most difficult part of the hive to make. They also offer a Top Bar Hive Package, which includes top bars, hive plans, spacers, and hardware. We find that having precise dimensions for the top bars encourages the bees to build straighter comb which leads to a better beekeeping experience in the hive.

They also suggest that you build the hive with the glass viewing window, this is an amazing feature that you will not want to leave out. The window allows you to observe the progress of the bees without having to disturb the colony. This also gives you the opportunity to check on your bees anytime you'd like.

2) FIND A RESOURCE FOR A SWARM, OR ORDER BEES

January or February is the time to order a package of bees or get onto a local swarm list. Bee Package Suppliers start selling their packages in the winter in preparation for a spring delivery of a package of bees. Bee Packages normally arrive in April, depending on your local climate. The weather needs to be warm enough for the bees to be put into a hive and there to be available nectar and pollen in your area for the bees to start collecting to feed their young they will start rearing. Bees start swarming in the spring. Most colonies will start swarming in April unless you are in a warmer region like the southern US and swarming can start as early as March.

3) PLACEMENT OF YOUR BEE HIVE

You will want to place the entrance of the hive away from foot traffic. The less foot traffic at the entrance of the hive the better for the bees, you and your friends. You'll need to consider the winter weather in your area and the direction of the wind. Face the hive entrance away from strong winter winds. The ideal direction would face somewhere between east and south. It is a good idea that the hive gets some shade in the afternoon in the summer and plenty of sun in the winter months. A great place for this is under a deciduous tree, where it is shaded in the afternoons in the summer, or on the east side of a building where the hive gets the warmth from the dawning sun and shade in the afternoon. You may also want to raise the hive off the ground a few feet so that it is easier to work with; a couple of cinder blocks works well for this. Level the hive, with the lid off, from front to back and from side to side. You may have to adjust the ground, or add shims under the feet of the hive.

4) PURCHASE PROTECTIVE CLOTHING FOR WORKING WITH THE HIVE.

Protective clothing means different things to different beekeepers.

When bees are being installed into the hive, they are not as aggressive or defensive as they can be once they have established. This means that they won't be concerned with stinging because they are concerned with finding their new home and colony. But you may want to wear a veil and protective clothing when first starting out with beekeeping.This helps you feel comfortable around the bees, allowing more concentration on your task.Purchase a bee suit, bee helmet and veil and protective gloves from our BackYardHive Protective Gear shop. You can also wear thick clothing, closing all arm and leg sleeves. Wrapping duck tape works well for this. And if you are in question about being allergic, you should get tested by your doctor.

5) COAT THE TOP BARS WITH MELTED DOWN BEESWAX

(paraffin will not work it needs to be natural bees wax) Coat only the 'spine' of the top bars. This encourages the bees to build comb on this 'spine'. You can order beeswax on our website or purchase it from your local art supply store.

6) INSTALL THE BEES INTO THE HIVE

Put all the top bars on the hive. Now it is time to install the bees into your hive. How many top bars you will need to remove and where you choose to put the false back, depends on the size of your swarm or colony. Typically, we suggest to insert your false back 10 bars from the front of the hive, this is important as it helps to establish the brood nest in the front of the hive. Remove 5 or more bars between the entrance and false back to install the bees into hive. If it's a package of bees the queen comes in a separate cage. Place this on top of the hive until the bees are installed in the hive. Give the box with the bees in it, a couple good stern shakes as you empty the bees into the hive. If needed give the box another stern shake, to get most of the bees into the hive. If the queen came in a cage you can put her into the hive with the bees; suspend the cage between the 3rd and 4th bars from the entrance. If you are installing a swarm make sure you locate the ball of bees on the lid of the box and carefully move the ball above the opening and give the top of the lid a stern pound, or shake. Then gently yet firmly shake the bees in the bottom part of the box into a corner, turn the box upside down and shake them into the hive. There will be bees flying all around.

Hopefully, most of them are in the hive. Put all but 1 bar back on the hive. Whether it's a package of bees you bought, or a feral swarm, you will want to make sure the queen is in the hive. They will soon start to fan, this is the bees calling out to each other "Hey, we are over here..the queen is here everyone get in!!" It can take about an hour or so for all the bees to find their way into the hive, replace your last top bar. In a couple of days, release the queen over the hive into the top of the hive, it is important that you do not drop her on the ground, so do all of your work over the hive where the top bars are removed so if she falls, she goes into her home. In 3-7 days move the false back all the way to the back of the hive, put in your spacers, and move the bees and combs 3 bars from the hive entrance, this will get the brood nest right where you want it.

WHAT HIVE TOOLS DO I NEED FOR WORKING WITH MY BEE HIVE?

Your hive tool is one of the essential pieces of beekeeping equipment you will need to work with your hive.If you only get one tool the ultimate Hive Toolspecially designed by Corwin Bell The ultimate Hive Tool that is versatile and the best choice for working your bee hive whether it is a top bar hive, Warre or Langstroth. An all-in-one sturdy hive tool for easily removing combs and prying apart top bars when working with your hive.

How Many Hives Can I Start At Once?

You can start as man hives as you feel comfortable managing. If you can build or buy more than hive it is a great idea to start with more than one hive as your learning curve doubles with 2 or more hives. Each hive will have a different personality and will have different traits like how fast they build combs, how much they guard the hive, how much they use propolis in their hive, the list goes on

How Far Apart Should My Bee Hives Be?

It is perfectly fine to put the hives in close proximity. Here are some things to think about.

1. You want enough room to walk between the hives and be able to work around each hive. The biggest problem for me has been when I am

harvesting honey in one hive and the adjacent hives' bees catch wind of the honey smell. I now have increased the number of bees landing on the combs I am trying to work. This is one reason I like to do the the single comb harvest with my hives that are close together. I can go in and remove a comb before any of the "other" bees get what's going on.

2. If the hives are close together they get used to each others' proximity and scent and let their guard down, which sometimes results in them robbing the other hive. Disease can more easily spread and infect hives in close proximity; this is much of the problem with big honey apiaries. I like to give the bees their own local territory. If you have the room I would put the hives several hundred feet away from each other. Otherwise 4 to 5 feet or enough room to walk between them and still be able to work the hive.

3. I get different honey from these hives.

A scenario might be; my #1 hive is right next to an apple tree will be a dark "apple honey" and the #2 hive, in the side-yard is going after the melon patch and the plum bushes across the road.

One of my favorite bee keeping joys is seeking out mono-flora areas. I drive and look for sunflower fields, different flowers down by a lake or fields with wild flowers. I will then put a hive in this area for a couple of months just to see what the flavor and color of the honey is.

Can I Install Two Hives At The Same Time?

If the hives are thirty feet away or more, you could install them at the same time, although thirty feet is really an arbitrary number - the main thing to consider is the time when the bees formed their colony and regrouped. When the first bees installed have stopped "fanning", then you can install the second colony of bees. Fanning is pretty neat to watch. The bees that are around the new hive will put their abdomens up in the air and rapidly fan the air. The bees are putting out pheromones and sonic vibrations signaling their buddies where the queen and the new hive are. So you can imagine if two colonies are doing this at the same time, it could be a little confusing.

1. Choose the location Bees need four things. First, they need sun, or afternoon shade if your weather is hot. Second, they must have access to fresh water near the hive. We used a large plant saucer with stones in the center for the bees to land on and refreshed the water every day. A shallow bubble fountain would work well, too. Third, the hive must be protected from wind, which can blow rain (or snow) into the hive, making it harder for the bees to keep the hive warm. Finally, bees need privacy. Don't put the hives near high-traffic areas, play areas, swimming pools, or pet areas. Give each hive plenty of space 50 feet from high-traffic areas is ideal, but if space is limited, position the hive so the entrance is near a tall fence or hedge. This will force their flight path overhead to minimize contact with people and pets. And screening them from view will keep bees and people happy.

2. Prepare the location Hives should face south, if possible, and they need to be kept off the ground to protect them from dampness and

critters. After clearing the brush and leveling the ground, we poured a cement pad to make care easier.

3. Install the bees Spring, when blooming flowers furnish a food supply, is the time to put your bees in their hives. Once you've chosen how to buy them, the best bet is to rely on your source for installation instructions.

Here is what happened when we picked up our bees from Randy Oliver at his property in Grass Valley: He gave us an introductory class in beekeeping, showing us how to use the hive tool and the smoker, handle bees, and check for eggs, brood (larvae), and queen all vital signs of a colony's health. Randy loaded 5 frames of his gentle hybrid bees and a queen into each of our two brood boxes and sealed the openings by stuffing them with our beekeeping gloves. We used ratchet straps to secure the boxes in the back of our truck. When we got back to Sunset, we positioned the brood boxes in their designated locations and removed the gloves from the entrances. One hive we named Betty; the other, Veronica.

4. Feed the bees Young colonies have a lot of work to do—storing pollen and nectar, sealing all the cracks and seams in their new home, and taking care of the queen and new brood. To make their adjustment easier, we fed them a "nectar." Here is how to make it: Dissolve equal parts granulated sugar and water and use to fill the quart jars. Top with the feeder lids and invert the jars into the holes. The lids should not drip;

they should be barely moist. The bees will drink what they need from the lids.

In the beginning, our nucs drank about three-fourths of a quart jar per day. Over the next 3 weeks or so, it tapered off to the point where we realized sugar water was no longer necessary. The bees were finding their nutrition in flowers. Plus, sugar water makes for insipid honey and should not be continued if it is not needed.

5. Inspect the hives inside and out Much of beekeeping is simple observation and response. If you are a novice beekeeper, inspect the hive about once a week for a couple of months so that you can learn. Once you feel comfortable, adjust your routine to every two weeks. Make sure the outside of the hive is clean and free of bee poop, the landing board is free of litter, and there are no ants on the hive. Open the hives and check frames for larvae and eggs (on warm days only). If the queen is healthy, you will see plenty of larvae in various stages of development.

If you don't see evidence of a healthy queen, consult an expert. Your local beekeeping guild is a good source.

Ultimately, the less often you inspect the hive, the better for its health. Opening the hives and thoroughly checking them requires smoking to keep the bees calm. This stresses the bees and it takes them about a day to recover. As you learn more, you will find you won't need to pull many frames to know what is going on inside. And you will figure out a lot simply by observing the bees as they come and go from the hive.

6. Check regularly for pests and diseases Varroa mites are the pest most typically found in hives. Left unchecked, they can cripple and eventually kill the hive (see Pest Control, below, for hints about checking for mites and mite control). Other pests you need to watch for include the small hive beetle and the wax moth. Diseases you need to be on the lookout for are American and European foulbrood. Early intervention can often mean the difference between a healthy hive and a dead hive.

7. Expand the hive when necessary Start with one deep hive body-brood box. When the bees have filled it with 7 or 8 frames of bees and brood, top it with a second brood box. Let the bees build up brood cells in the second brood box, too. When the second brood box is well filled (7 or 8 frames of bees), top it with a queen excluder, if you choose to use one, and, finally, the honey super (the box from which you will collect most of your honey).

Flying honeybees

A hive with a low colony count may struggle to defend invasions that can occur via large openings. These weak hives can benefit from entrance reducers.Beekeepers use t hese small blocks of wood to protect the hive from robbing honey bees or yellow jackets. While these add-ons aren't reccomended during the height of a honey flow, they can be helpful during winter to discourage drafts, rain, snow, and mice from entering the hive.

PEST CONTROL

Bees are like flying balls of delicate spun sugar filled with honey. Everything wants to eat them. Here are three of the worst pests we battled, and the tactics we used.

Ants Argentine ants can kill a hive by robbing honey and eating the brood. We couldn't spray to kill the ants, since that would also kill the bees. We tried Terro ant bait little containers filled with boric acid mixed with a sweet substance ants like with some success. In the end, we were most successful with a physical barrier. We placed each leg of the hive stands in plastic tubs filled with water that the ants could not cross.

Small hive beetles Hive beetle larvae will eat all parts of the hive, including the baby bees. We kill the beetles on site, and have been experimenting with traps like AJs Beetle Eater ($5.25) from Dadant.

Varroa mites The most damaging pests a beekeeper has to deal with are these mites, as they threaten the survival of a hive once they become established. They suck the blood of adult bees and lay their eggs in brood cells, where their larvae feed off bee babies, infecting them with viruses and weakening and even killing them. To save their bees, beekeepers use a variety of methods:

1. **Monitoring** A 24-hour count of a natural mite fall will give you a good idea of a hive's infestation. Coat the bottom of your Country Rube board with petroleum jelly or cooking spray (to trap the mites), slide it into the lower part of the bottom board, wait for 24 hours, and then pull it out and count the mites. Anything more than 10 mites per brood box indicates you have a problem.

2. **Sugar dusting** The powdered sugar method lets you both count the mites and control them. Sift powdered sugar, 1 cup per brood box, over the tops of the frames and brush it into the hive. The powdered sugar makes the mites lose their grip on the bees and fall off; plus the bees groom the sugar off their bodies, dislodging more mites. Again, use the bottom board to capture the fallen mites. You should not see more than a few mites 10 minutes after dusting. If there are more, you have a problem.

3. **Mite trapping** Drone frames will also help trap varroa mites. These frames are designed to encourage bees to make drone comb cells, which are larger than worker comb cells. Since varroa mites prefer drone brood 10 to 1, the drone comb makes a great mite trap. Just before the drones hatch (24 days after the eggs were laid), destroy the drone comb (you can freeze it and return it to the hive, or simply cut it out), and replace the drone frame for the next cycle. (Since our queens have already mated and have a lifetime's supply of sperm inside of them, they do not need the drones in order to reproduce.)

4. **Apiguard** A gel infused with thymol, made from the oils of thyme plants. It works well, but it makes the honey stored during the treatment taste like mouthwash.

5. Formic acid More toxic than thymol, formic acid kills the mites by gassing them. It makes the honey inedible for humans, so it is applied in the fall and winter, when the nectar flow is slow or stopped. You need to wear a respirator when applying it.

HONEY COLLECTION

We were lucky to collect honey the first summer. Typically, during the first year the bees build up their hive, and if they overwinter well, you can begin harvesting in the late spring or early summer of the second year. Three months after bringing our bees home, we had 4 frames packed with honey, each weighing about 8 pounds. Lacking a professional extractor, we used the following low-tech method.

1. Cut and crush Using the bench scraper, we cut the honey wax and all off the foundation into a bowl, balancing the frame on a wooden spoon set across the bowl like a bridge. Then we used a wooden spoon to crush the honey and wax in the bowl.

2. Straining and settling We poured this slurry of wax and honey through a double layer of cheesecloth and the stainless-steel strainer into our food-grade plastic bucket. Then we left it to drain and settle for a couple of days (bubbles and foam rose to the surface).

3. Bottling We covered the floor with newspapers and got our jars ready. Then we loosened the honey gate (the stopper at the bottom of the bucket) to release the honey into each jar.In went the honey, on went the lids.It was as simple as that. From 4 full frames of honeycomb, we reaped 12 pounds, 10 ounces of honey. We rinsed the leftover wax and froze it. Later, we rendered the wax in a solar wax melter and used it for craft projects like lip balm and hand salve. We had a second surprise harvest later in the summer, bringing our total to about 31 pounds of pure, fragrant honey.

HONEY BEES FOR SALE

A FEW POINTS TO CONSIDER BEFORE YOU BUY

If you are starting beekeeping, no doubt you will be looking out for honey bees for sale. But how should you make your choice?

Firstly, if you are establishing a colony, you will probably purchase a nucleus colony or a 'nuc'. A nuc consists of a queen, brood, and workers in four or more frames.

Alternatively you may purchase package bees, which will consist of workers and a newly mated queen, and food.

Before purchasing, here are a few considerations:

- The bees should of course be disease free.

- Where do they come from – which race/sub-species of honey bee are they? Some suppliers import queens from overseas, but some beekeepers prefer to purchase queens reared in their own country to minimise the risk of bringing in new strains of virus or disease. Ask the supplier for details.

- Temperament - if this is your first time beekeeping, and you are nervous, then you may prefer to choose 'mild mannered' bees.

Note there are additional circumstances when you may wish to purchase honey bees, such as the replacement of winter losses.

More considerations

Timing

Note that if you wish to buy bees, you may have to order in advance so that you don't miss out. Ensure you have everything set up to and ready for your bees before you receive them. Also, have a good supply of food for the bees, until they settle and begin their normal foraging.

Take a look at my lists of bee plants to ensure you have a good range of nectar and pollen available in your garden for the bees throughout the seasons. If you live in an urban area, there may be plenty of flowering plants in the vicinity, from gardens and public planting schemes.

Swarms

What if you are offered a swarm? If you are a newcomer to beekeeping, you may want to get help from another beekeeper to settle in the swarm into your hive.

Where Else Can I Get Honey Bees?

- Make contacts with your local beekeeping association, who may be alerted to the locations of swarms that need to be moved.

- Contact your local council, and let them know you are wanting a swarm. If a member of the public asks to have a swarm removed, they can then contact you.

WHERE TO GET BEES

Packaged bees and caged queen It takes time to build up the colony this way, but it's the least-expensive choice. You can usually order packaged bees through your local beekeepers' guild.Preorder as early as the fall and certainly no later than early spring, as bees are only available for a short time in spring.About $65.

Nuc (short for "nucleus") A nuc is a young hive, usually covering no more than 5 frames of comb, with a newly laying queen. Starting this way helps you get a jump on honey production.Buy from a reputable beekeeper to avoid getting diseased equipment or sick bees.We ordered two nucs from master beekeeper Randy Oliver and drove to his location in Grass Valley, California, to pick them up.$90 for each nuc, queen included; scientificbeekeeping.com.

Well established swarms or colonies Large colonies can be daunting if you've never kept bees before, and beginning beekeepers shouldn't try to capture a swarm. Leave that to a more experienced beekeeper (contact your local beekeepers' guild to find such a person), and perhaps he or she will help you start a hive with the captured swarm.

BEE ACTIVITY BY SEASON

Each season brings its own challenges to a hive and the bees react accordingly. The activity level of a bee is dictated by the weather and cold weather inhibits their movement. In fact, bees left out in the elements, unprotected will often not survive the winter.

A high-level concentration of bees in a beehive will be better able to tolerate the cold than a hive with fewer bees. But any hive is in danger of succumbing to the cold if the temperature drops too low. Your role is to act as custodian of the hive, keeping it safe and in good condition throughout the year. The rest is up to the bees!

Winter

During the winter, the bees will form a tight cluster around the queen to ensure her survival and keep each other as protected as possible during the coldest months. Only female worker bees will be in the hive at this point, having forced out the drones who no longer serve any purpose.

The bees will eat about 50 pounds of honey during this period, but will run out of food before the winter weather eases. You will need to provide the hive with sugar to supplement their appetites toward the end of the season. In the meantime, your main objective is to keep snow and ice off the hive and ensure there is an emergency food supply available.

Of course, since bees will be confined to a hive, starting a beehive in the winter makes no sense.

Spring

Honeybees will often begin spring close to starvation, and so you will often need to provide an emergency food supply until the flowers begin to bloom and the bees begin to harvest their own food supply again.

If you are starting a beehive in the spring, it is generally necessary to help the bees by feeding them sugar syrup. This will help them build resources inside the hive until they are able to find a supply of foraging resources in the area, at which point they will hopefully become self-sufficient.

As the weather warms up, the queen will more produce eggs and their food stores will gradually replenish. You should monitor the bees to make sure that everything is going according to plan and that they are producing adequate food for themselves. It may be necessary to supply them with them with emergency food rations until you observe that they have an adequate food source of their own.

By May, the activity in the hive should be in full swing and the drones that were eliminated when winter began will have been largely replaced. You should maintain your normal beekeeping routines at this time, including medicating the colony and adding more supers as the need for them arises. This period may see an explosion in the hive population, so be sure to keep up with the maintenance of the hive.

Summer

June and July see the worker bees in constant motion collecting pollen, producing honey and tending to the queen. The drones will be thickest through this period, but you will see their population begin to diminish in August as their usefulness to the queen wanes.

Be mindful of predators and other insects that may be attracted to the honey and may cause damage to the hive or the bees. As September begins, the drones' presence will drastically change and you will see the population of the hive decline as the drones are dismissed by the worker bees.

Fall

At this point, you will probably have harvested the hive's honey, but be sure to leave around 60-70 pounds of honey for the bees to survive the harsh months ahead. The queen will lay fewer eggs now as the workers' activity begins to die down.

This is when the beekeeper should medicate the bees and supplement their food with sugar syrup. As fall progresses, the bees will begin to huddle around the queen and there will be little activity from them. You should use this time to reinforce the security of the hive to keep out rodents and predators that will make a meal out of a hibernating brood colony.

November and December will call for little more than cursory inspections to make sure that everything is as it should be.

Weather Conditions for a New Hive

When spring begins and the weather begins to warm is the ideal time for bees to start a new hive. Their activity levels build along with the blooming of flowers and they can tend to and build their hive as the season flourishes. Cold weather will inhibit the bees' movements and they will not work on the hive until the season changes. Spring may begin later in some regions than others, so you should plan for your specific region.

Timing to Start in the Spring

When starting a beehive, the spring is ideal time. As soon as the weather begins to warm up and flowers start to bloom, you can set up your hive. Plan well and get your bees into the hive as soon as possible to allow them the time to gather as much nectar as possible through the next few months. By the time fall rolls around, the hive should be well established and honey should have been produced in abundance, barring any unforeseen complications.

When To Order Bees

You need to order your bees to arrive in early spring to get them installed in the hive on time. Ordering and receipt of your bees are two different things! Be sure to order well in advance to ensure your bees do indeed arrive on time. Talk to local beekeepers to identify the optimum time to order from local suppliers.

Don't jump the gun and accept delivery before the weather warms up in your area (obviously this differs across the country). You want the bees roused enough to begin building the hive and making it their own quickly. For beginners, do careful research on when your region will ring in the spring fully and prepare for your hive from there.

FEEDING HONEY BEES FOR BEGINNERS

In my first year of beekeeping. I was surprised to learn how often I had to feed my new pets. I wasn't supposed to be amazed, like all the livestock that honey bees have to consume.

Unfortunately, I've done a lot of reading on the Internet and heard that feeding your bees is bad—unnatural, unhealthful, makes them lazy, and swarm, can make them produce brood at the wrong time, etc, etc... Anyway, if you don't take too much honey out of them, they won't have to be fed. Well, that last declaration may be true—in a nice year, with a well developed nest. But not in most years in Mid TN, and definitely not for the first year of hives that have not yet been developed.

In My Opinion, ensuring that your bees—or your dog, bird, or children—have a good nutritional year around is essential to maintaining them healthy and efficient.

Yes natural fruit and honey may be more perfect plant food than milk and pollen, but inform me that you'd let your children starve because new fruit is out of season and canned beans are not perfect? Well, how about your dog? There is not a lot of dog chow accessible in nature?

So assuming that we agree that you sometimes need to feed your bees, we're mostly speaking about simple ancient table sugar in one shape or another. Store on it, and watch for sales 4-5 pound packages are often cheaper, and easier than bulk sugar until you have a few hives. But always hold a few of them on side just in emergencies.

How do you understand when you want to feed?

Very simple. Do your inspections. Any hive that does not produce at least 15 pounds of honey and free flowers mixed with nice quantities of both should be supplied. Starting around mid-September, this amount shifts to 50 pounds of healed "honey"and strong sugar. Once those things are achieved, you can avoid feeding until they use some of them and need to be supplied again. Which you'll understand because you're supposed to do the inspection.

While doing your checks, you need to look out for the backfilling of the brood nest if you see the flowers placed in the brood nest, then stop eating and stay vigilant. Allowing backfilling to proceed either because you're eating, or because of a natural water stream will lead in swarming if it lasts for just a few days. In addition to not eating, you can also offer them more blank drawn comb to function with or open the family shed by inserting a baseless frame the comb will be built in it and the woman will put eggs in the fresh comb. Both of these operations assist stop swarming.

Luckily, there is usually plenty of pollen available in our area almost any time the bees can forage so you don't really need to worry about using pollen replacements in your first year. But 1 caution just in case you decide to test the hot climate pollen sub particularly in the shape of "patties" is generally very rapidly infested with insect larvae.

What kind of feeder should I use?

Inverted quart containers or in the drop when I use reversed 2 gallon pails so I can get the work accomplished a lot faster. Cheap. Don't destroy the bees. They're also putting the feed directly on top of the bees where they can get it even in hot climates. You can either put it on top of the hive if it has a hole in the cover how I do it over a hole in the inner cover, enclosed in an empty super, or directly over the top bars. If you're using jars, don't let the sun shine on them heat the product and spread it to the hive cover it with an open super, coffee can, aluminum foil anything to hold the immediate sun off.

Miller feeders are popular easy to complete, and they retain a ton of food. Expensive and generally some bees drown. If you put them on during the summer, they may be stuffed with a comb.

Boardman feeders—not advised because they can break the robbery off.

Frame feeders they need to open the nest to eat, swallow some birds but they're putting the feed where they can get it even in hot climates.

Ziplock baggies—cheap one-use solution—don't destroy bees if they're finished properly. They don't have a lot of food, and they need to open the hive to change you can't refill it.

WHAT TO FEED BEEN IN THE HIVE

Honey bees store honey in the hive to provide food for winter and for other times when there are few or no nectar secreting flowers available.

When nectar is in short supply or unavailable, bees draw on their honey stores in the hive. During these times, it is important to frequently monitor the amount of honey in the hive because when it has all gone, the colony will starve.

Starvation can be prevented by moving bees to an area where plants are yielding nectar or by feeding them white table sugar, or syrup made with white sugar. Never use raw, brown and dark brown sugar, and molasses as these may cause dysentery in bees. Bee colonies can be kept alive for long periods by feeding white sugar.

HONEY AS FEED FOR BEES

It is extremely important not to feed honey to bees unless it is from your own disease free hives. Spores of American foulbrood disease can be present in honey. Feeding honey from an unknown source, for example, a supermarket or even another beekeeper, may cause infection in your hives. If you feed suitable honey to your bees, it must be placed inside the hive. Never place honey in the open outside the hive as this is illegal under the Livestock Disease Control Act 1994.

How And When To Feed Bees

If sugar syrup or dry sugar is fed in the open, bees from nearby managed and feral colonies will be attracted. You will end up feeding other bees as well as your own. Besides being a waste of money, feeding in the open may cause robber bee activity in the apiary and possible interchange of bee disease pathogens.

Placement of sugar syrup or dry sugar in hives is best done towards evening to minimise any tendency for bees to rob the hives that are fed.

MAKING AND FEEDING SUGAR SYRUP

There are differing views about the correct amount of sugar in syrup. Some beekeepers prefer a ratio of one part of sugar to one part of water, measured by weight (known as 1:1). Others prefer a dense syrup of two parts of sugar to one part of water (known as 2:1). Generally, 1:1 syrup is used to supplement honey stores, stimulate colonies to rear brood and encourage drawing of comb foundation particularly in spring. The stronger syrup is used to provide food when honey stores in the hive are low. Measuring the sugar and water by weight or volume is alright because there is no need to be 100% exact about the sugar concentration.

Heat the water in a container large enough to hold both the water and sugar. As soon as the water has begun to boil gently, remove the container from the heat source. Pour in the sugar and stir the mixture until the sugar crystals are dissolved. Never boil the mixture as the sugars may caramelise and may be partially indigestible and toxic to bees.

Always let the syrup cool to room temperature before feeding it to bees. The cooled syrup can be given to hives using one of the following four methods.

Container with sealable lid

Fill a clean jar, tin with a push-down lid, or similar container with sugar syrup. Drill or punch the lid with 6-8 very small holes. Cut two 12 mm high risers from a piece of wood and place them across the top bars of the frames that are in the top box of the hive. Invert the filled container and place it on the risers. Next, place an empty super on the hive to enclose the feeder and then replace the hive lid. The risers provide a bee space between the top bars and the holes in the container lid. It is a good idea to remove the cardboard insert commonly found in jar lids.

Plastic bag

Partially fill a plastic freezer bag with sugar syrup, about half full. Gently squeeze the bag to expel all the air. Tie the neck of the bag using an elastic band. Place the bag on the top bars of the frames in the top box of the hive, under the hive cover. Use a brad or very small diameter nail to punch about 6-8 small holes into the upper surface of the bag. The bees will suck the syrup through the holes. Never put the holes on the under surface of the bag as the syrup may leak out faster than the bees can gather it. This may lead to loss of syrup outside the hive and cause robbing by nearby bees. It is important to have a bee space between the upper surface of the bag and the under surface of the hive lid so the bees can gain access to the syrup. If required, a wooden riser of the dimensions of the hive may be used to raise the lid.

Shallow tray

Place sugar syrup in a shallow tray, such as aluminium foil tray, under the hive lid. Bees need to be able to reach the syrup without falling into the liquid and drowning. Some grass straw or wood straw of the type used in cooling devices may be placed in the syrup for this purpose. It is important not use any straw or floating that has been treated, or been in contact, with chemicals as this may be hazardous to bees. The hives should be on level ground to prevent loss of syrup and a riser may need to be used if the tray is not shallow.

Frame feeder

Place sugar syrup in a 'frame or division board feeder'. This is a container, the size of a full-depth Langstroth frame, that has an open top and which sits in the super as a normal frame does. The feeder requires a flotation material or other means to allow bees to access the syrup without drowning.

How Often To Feed

It is normal for bees to remove syrup from a feeder, reduce the water content and store it in the combs as if it were honey. Whatever feeder is used, a medium to strong colony will usually empty it in a matter of days.

For colonies with virtually no stored honey and no incoming nectar, the initial feed will be largely determined by the amount of brood, the size of the colony and to some degree, the size of the container used to hold the syrup. It is safer to over-feed a colony than to skimp and possibly cause the death of the colony. Some beginners have tried tablespoons of syrup, but this amount is much too small. An initial feed of around 1-3 litres could be tried. It is then important to frequently check the combs to see how much syrup has been stored. This will give a guide as to how often and how much syrup should be given. Feeding can be stopped when nectar becomes available.

Properly ripened syrup should have a moisture content of around 18%. Syrup that is not ripened adequately will ferment and adversely affect bees. Colonies with insufficient stores for winter should be given enough syrup to boost their stores before the cold weather of autumn sets in. This will enable the bees to fully process the syrup.

Feeding dry sugar

Medium to strong colonies can also be fed dry white table sugar placed on hive mats or in trays under the hive lid. Bees require water for liquefying the sugar crystals. They will obtain supplies from sources outside the hive and sometimes use condensation that may occur inside the hive. Some beekeepers prefer to wet the sugar with water to prevent it from solidifying. In effect, this creates a partial syrup. Weak colonies may be incapable of gathering sufficient water and feeding of dry sugar to them is not recommended. Regardless of colony size, feeding dry sugar works best during autumn and spring when humidity is relatively high. The hot, dry conditions of summer make it hard for bees to dissolve sugar crystals into a liquid.

It may be preferable for a colony at starvation level to be first fed syrup before dry sugar is given. This will give the bees immediate food without the need to liquefy crystals. Bees will generally not use dry sugar when they are able to collect sufficient nectar for the colony's needs. The sugar will remain in the hive and in some cases will be deposited by the bees outside the hive entrance. A small amount of dry sugar may be converted to liquid and stored in the cells.

Important note

Sugar remaining in combs must not be extracted with the next honey crop. The sugar will contaminate the honey and the extracted product will not conform to the legal standards set out in the Australia New Zealand Food Standards Code - Standard 2.8.2 – Honey. Ideally, the amount of sugar that was given to the hive will be fully eaten by the bees at the time hives are placed on a honey flow. This is not always possible to achieve. Also, during expansion of the brood nest, sugar stored in brood nest combsmay be moved by the bees to the honey super.

When To Stop Feeding Bees

Never feed bees sugar water when honey collection supers are on the hive. I am referring to boxes of honey that are intended for human consumption.

The bees will use any nectar (or nectar-like substance) to make honey. Honey or honeycomb produced from sugar water instead of nectar that's a no no. And, its not real honey.

Established colonies can usually survive on their own unless you are in a drought. New colonies need extra help.

BEEKEEPING KITS WITH JAR FEEDERS

Each year, new beekeepers begin their adventure with beekeeping kits. Perhaps, they ordered the kit for themselves or maybe it was a gift.

Beekeeping kits can be a good purchase depending on the quality of items included. Beware of beekeeping kits that come with small jar feeders.

The small jar bee feeders can be a hazard in the hands of inexperienced beekeepers. They make look cute hanging on the front of the hive but should only be used inside the hive.

Let me repeat that as it is very important Jar Beehive Feeders should only be used INSIDE a hive. This is especially true if you have more than 1 hive in the location.

A kit without a feeder is a better value for most new beekeepers. Then, you can choose the style of feeder that you would like to use.

Jar Bee Feeders you Need More than 1

Quart jar feeders can be done with materials at home or you can purchase the jar holders also called Entrance Feeders or Boardman Feeders.

If made at home, sugar water is mixed well and poured into the glass jars. Granulated cane sugar is the sugar of choice when making bee sugar water.

Using a small nail, punch several tiny holes in the metal jar lid. When inverted and placed on the hive, bees will access sugar water through the small holes.

If placed directly on the top bars of the hive, you will need an extra deep box to enclose the feeder.

Some beekeepers use a temporary hive top with a 1" – 2" hole in the top. (You can use a wide drill bit to do this.) The upside-down jar is placed over the hole.

Be sure to secure the jar to the hive in some way.i.e. Cover it with a plastic bucket and place a brick on top etc.

We do not want the wind or a raccoon to push the jar over. Of course, you can also use an empty deep box (with a top) to enclose jars inside the hive.

A Tip for Jar Bee Feeders

One easy way to use jar feeders is to purchase or make 4 jars feeders. Place all 4 inside the hive sitting on the inner cover.

Use an extra deep hive box to enclose the jars and then put the top back on the hive. This allows the bees to have access to a gallon of sugar water inside the hive.

Bees Should Not Need Constant Feeding

Nectar availability ebbs and flows in most areas. It is subject to climate conditions such as drought or a late freeze.

Strong winds, cold temperatures or rain can affect foraging conditions. If the population of your beehive is small, you do not have as many workers to collect nectar.

Too little food during Spring build up causes the bees to sacrifice brood or baby bees. Poor foraging conditions in the Fall prevents storage of food for Winter survival.

The bottom line is that we cant always rely on natural nectar. This is especially true because we keep more hives in a one area than you would find in nature.

Feeding Honey Bees Sugar Water for New Colonies

Let's talk about package bees. The majority of new bee hives established each year begin with package bees.

This small wooden and screen box contains about 10,000 bees and a queen. Other than a small can of sugar water, the bees have no resources but themselves.

Experienced beekeepers often freeze excess frames of honey. These are fed back to colonies at a later time. Unfortunately, the new beekeeper does not have this option.

Feeding honey bees sugar water is necessary in most areas. Checkout my post on feeding package bees .

What to Use for Bee Syrup or Sugar Water

I prefer sugar water made with pure cane sugar. Avoid powered sugar, brown sugar, molasses etc when feeding bees. These sugars have indigestible components that can make your bees sick.

If the bag does not say pure cane sugar, it probably is not. You should be able to find pure cane sugar in your local grocery but you can order it if you prefer.

Some beekeepers, especially those with a large number of hives use regular granulated sugar. It is most likely made from beets. This should work well as far as we know there are some concerns about beet sugar. How to Make Sugar

#1 Problem New Beekeepers Face When Feeding Honey Bees Sugar WaterThere are 2 basic recipes for sugar water used by beekeepers.

We call them 1:1 (1 to 1) and 2:1 (2 to 1) ratio.

Let's break this down because to a new beekeeper it can be so confusing.

You can measure by weight or volume it does not matter. New colonies are fed 1:1 to encourage brood rearing. 2:1 (2 parts sugar to 1 part water) is used in the fall to encourage storage of food for winter.

Sugar water honey will keep your colony from starvation but it is not real honey. A golden rule to remember when feeding bees sugar water.

Remember, never feed bees when honey supers on your colony are meant for human consumption.

Many beekeepers use a feeding supplement in their sugar water. It promotes good feeding and prevents your syrup from becoming moldy.

Containing essential oils, these products are reported to promote good health in our bee colonies.

These products are concentrated add only a small amount to the sugar water for your bees.

Honey Bee Feeders

A multitude of feeders are available for feeding honey bees sugar water. Each type or method has pros and cons. Lets explore the most common bee feeders.

A Boardman Feeder (Entrance Feeder)

Use this feeder with a regular glass canning jar. It fits into the front hive entrance. A beekeeper can easily see when to refill.

But, this type of feeder does have its problems. It does not hold a lot of sugar water and will require refilling often. A hungry colony can drain this in a couple of hours.

The smell will attract wasps and bees from other hives to the entrance. This may result in fighting and robbing.

If you want to use a boardman feeder, place it inside the hive. The entrance feeder can be placed on top of the frames needs an empty box around it to close up the hive. You can use several feeders at one time!

The Hive Top Feeder

Hive top feeders sit on top of the hive under the telescoping top. They may be made of wood or plastic. This is a great option for the new beekeeper who is not able to visit their hives daily.

The feeder will hold around 1-2 gallons of bee syrup and will feed the colony for several days. One disadvantage of hive top feeders is their tendency to leak over time.

They are also heavy when filled and care must be taken to avoid spilling syrup around the hive.

Frame Feeders

A frame feeder takes the place of one frame in the hive body. Most frame feeders hold approximately 1 gallon of syrup. Being inside the hive, the bees have easy access to the food.

Frame feeders have some cons. You have to open the hive to refill. And, you will always have some bees drown in the feeder.

If you choose to use frame feeders, put some type of floating material inside. I have used small sticks or wooden Popsicle sticks to reduce bee drowning.

Open Feeding Sugar Water

This methods for feeding bees has some merits but it is also risky. Honey bees drown very easy. Also, it is not an economical way to feed. You are feeding every bee and wasp in the neighborhood.

If you do plan to try open feeding, ensure that the feeders are well away from your hives. At least 50 feet, more is better or you increase the risk of creating a robbing frenzy.

Bucket Feeders (Or Pail Feeders)

The bucket feeder is one of the most popular bee feeders. A small plastic bucket with a mesh feeder hole holds 1 gallon of sugar syrup. (You will also find larger styles available.)

Fill the bucket with sugar syrup. Put the lid on tightly. When you turn the bucket upside down, some syrup will escape until a vacuum forms.

Put the upside down bucket directly on top of the frames. Bees will feed from the mesh feeder hole in the bucket (or small holes drilled by the manufacturer).

Like the boardman feeders, this method requires extra equipment. An empty hive body around the bucket allows the hive to be closed.

If you choose, you can use a temporary hive top with a small hole drilled in the center.

Place your upturned bucket over the hole. A brick or rock on top of the bucket will prevent wind damage.

Refilling the bucket can be accomplished easily without disturbing the colony. And no drowned bees !

Outside feeding is interesting to watch but it causes frenzy activity. Never use outside feeders near your hives!

The biggest mistake made by new beekeepers is failing to feed a new colony long enough. Feeding honey bees sugar water can not have a set time frame of when to stop.

When bees first arrive, they are hungry and feed heavily. In a few weeks, a natural nectar flow (or honey flow) may occur in your area.

When attempting to buy honey bees, we often want bees that will be delivered right before this time.

A beekeeper who stops feeding in April may find a surprise in the September hive. No food stores for winter and frames that do not have honeycomb drawn out are common.

The new colony full of potential in the spring now faces starvation.

The moral of this story is feed your bees. If they lose interest in the sugar syrup, remove it for a few weeks. Then offer a small amount of food. If they take it quickly, you will know it is time to start feeding again.

You should stop once they colony has drawn out the comb in all your frames and filled some with honey. (How much will depend on your climate. In my area, I want a deep and a shallow full by September.

FEEDING SUGAR WATER IN WINTER – NO

If you have colonies that need additional Winter stores, feed them while the weather is warm. Bees can not make good use of sugar syrup in cold temperatures.

Preventing Robbing When Feeding Bees

I love my bees but they are all little "robbers and thieves" . Especially during times of a nectar shortage or complete lack of nectar (we call that a dearth)you may experience robbing.

The stronger or more aggressive hives with fight the weaker hive and steal honey(sugar water). Once this begins it is difficult to stop.

If you see a fighting frenzy at the front of your hive, cover the hive with a damp towel. The towel hanging down loosely over the entrance of the hive tends to calm the situation.

If that is not successful, I have turned a water sprinkler on the hive for a few hours.

Robbing is best avoided. Be vigilant when feeding bees, keep entrances small enough for the colony to defend.

If a small colony, entrance should be only about 1 inch, a larger colony of strong nuc can have a bit larger opening.

Feeding bees is a lot of work and expense. How much you need to feed will depend on your climate and foraging conditions.

HONEY BEE SWARMING

Swarming is a natural process in the life of a honey bee colony. Swarming occurs when a large group of honey bees leaves an established colony and flies off to establish a new colony, essentially creating two from one. Swarming is a natural method of propagation that occurs in response to crowding within the colony. Swarming usually occurs in late spring and early summer and begins in the warmer hours of the day.

Honey bee swarms may contain several hundred to several thousand worker bees, a few drones and one queen. Swarming bees fly around briefly and then cluster on a tree limb, shrub or other object. Clusters usually remain stationary for an hour to a few days, depending on weather and the time needed to find a new nest site by scouting bees. When a suitable location for the new colony, such as a hollow tree, is found the cluster breaks up and flies to it.

Honey bee swarms are not highly dangerous under most circumstances.Swarming honey bees feed prior to swarming, reducing their ability to sting. Further, bees away from the vicinity of their nest (offspring and food stores) are less defensive and are unlikely to sting unless provoked.

In most situations when a honey bee swarm is found on a tree, shrub or house you do not need to do anything. Swarms are temporary and the bees will move on if you patiently ignore them. Stay back and keep others away from the swarm, but feel free to admire and appreciate the bees from a safe distance.

Only if a serious health threat is present because of the location of the swarm, such as in a highly traveled public area, should you attempt to do anything with a swarm. Only as a last resort, you can spray a swarm of bees with soapy water (up to 1 cup of liquid dishwashing detergent in a gallon of water) to kill the bees. Spraying a honey bee swarm is a risky operation because of the large number of bees.

COLD TEMPERATURE AND HONEY BEES

Winter HiveHoney bees will keep the inside temperature of the cluster at about 95 degrees by shivering and expending energy. A bee does not die until its body temperature is 41 degrees. At 41 degrees the bee can't operate or flex it's shivering muscles to stay warm.

The honey bee can survive cold temperature better than wind. It is the wind that is most harmful. Windchill is the single most harmful factor that results in bee deaths in cold climates. If a beehive is located in a shelter or a suitable wind block is supplied, the hives have the best chance for survival.

Last year, the windchill rather than cold temperature correlated significantly with honey bee losses. Windchill is not considered by USDA as a factor when determining honey bee losses. According to USDA, a claim for honey bee losses is not paid unless the temperature does not rise above 14 degrees for 7 consecutive days. On the Island, we should see 20 degrees by Sunday. We have sustained 6 consecutive days where the temperature has not been above 14 degrees, so a claim for losses will not be covered so far this year.

Our location suffered the coldest winter in 70 years but unfortunately, our 2013/2014 losses were not covered by the Emergency Livestock Assistance Program, (ELAP) since our location experienced only 5 days that met the criteria. No losses were covered because most of the winter the cold vacillated between negative temperatures and just above 14 degrees.

Outside the Hive

Often times a honey bee, on its flight back from collecting nectar or pollen, will stop along the way. This is not because the bee is tired and needs a rest. This is the result of flying at 12-15 miles per hour with the wind velocity cooling the bee. The bee stops to flex its flight muscles to warm up.

Bees are cold blooded and there is a limit to the amount of heat they can generate by metabolizing honey and exercising their wing muscles. Clearly, they can stay warm enough when active at outside temperatures in the low 40's, but the warmth will dissipate fairly quickly at colder temperatures and as activity decreases.

I frequently see my Russian bees in flight and gathering nectar on 40 degree days whereas Italians and Carnolians require 50-57 degree days. This is why Russians are cold hardy.

HOW LONG DO HONEY BEES LIVE?

The life span of honey bees varies, depending on the role of an individual bee within the colony. Honey bees live in sophisticated, well organised colonies - they are 'superorganisms'. A honey bee colony could comprise between 50,000 and 60,000 bees, performing different roles in order to help ensure the smooth running and success of the colony.

The role of a bee, as well as the time of year in which it was born (spring/summer or autumn), is also a factor in the lifespan for worker bees in the colony. Worker bees born in spring/summer have shorter, busier lives, whilst those born in autumn may live longer, but they must survive the harsher winter conditions to emerge from the hive the following spring.

In summary:

Queen Honey Bees

All being well, a honey bee queen could live for 3 to 4 years, as long as she is free from disease. It can even be longer - some beekeepers report queen survival of up to 6 years. This is much longer than bumble bee queens or the solitary bee species.

However, a queen that is no longer favoured by the colony may be removed by the workers. In such a case, a new queen will be produced, and the old queen replaced. This is called 'supersedure'. In some beekeeping practices, the queen is replaced by the beekeeper after one or two years.

The bumblebee queen is the founder of new bumblebee colonies.....

The bumblebee queen will emerge from hibernation, already impregnated from the previous year, and will then begin to feed. Nectar will provide her with much needed energy, whilst pollen will give protein, and help her ovaries to develop.

She will then begin the important endeavour of finding a suitable nest site. You may see them early in the year, zig-zagging low across the grass, exploring banks and hedgerow bottoms, and possibly bumping into windows as they try to find a suitable place to establish a nest and rear a colony.

Nest sites, due to habitat destruction, have become increasingly scarce, and it is believed queens will even fight over suitable sites.

Once a suitable nest site has been found, the queen will then begin to establish her colony. Seeing a queen bumblebee carrying pollen loads on her legs is a signal that the establishment of a colony is now underway.

The queen bumblebee is larger than the workers and males she produces. Unlike the female workers, she has the ability to control the sex of the eggs she lays through the use of a chemical signal (pheromone). Worker bumblebees can produce eggs too, but their offspring will be male bees only.

Queens will sometimes face competition from cuckoo bumblebees. Cuckoos attempt to take over a nest, sometimes (but not always) killing the resident queen if successful.

Unlike the host, cuckoo species are unable to carry pollen and secrete wax to make cells.

At the end of the season, only the newly emerged queen bumblebees will survive (although there are some exceptions in warm climates). They will mate, and hibernate to establish new colonies the following year. New queens emerge from colonies toward the end of the season, and begin feeding to lay down fat reserves ready for hibernation. In truth, a colony can only be deemed successful if it has had the opportunity to successfully produce queens that can mate and hibernate, and thus ensure future generations.

Quick Facts About The Honey Bee Queen

The honey bee queen is the largest of the bees in a honey bee (Apis mellifera) colony, measuring around 2 cm - that's about twice the length of a worker - drones are slightly larger than workers.

For the human eye, despite being larger than the workers, honey bee queens are difficult to spot among thousands and thousands of worker bees. For this reason, beekeepers mark queens with a dot of special paint on the thorax, as can be seen in the photograph above.

As she establishes her colony, she may lay 1000 eggs per day – one egg every 20 seconds - and more than her own body weight in eggs!

If a queen is not performing very well (for example, if she is not laying enough eggs), the colony may decide to replace her with a new queen. This is called supersedure.

In a colony of 50,000 bees, there will be only 1 queen, and perhaps around 300 drones (males) and the rest will be female worker honey bees. At exceptional times, there may temporarily be 2 queens, but not for very long. More about this below.

HOW ARE QUEEN HONEY BEES DIFFERENT FROM WORKERS?

Apart from being significantly larger than workers, the roles that queens perform is very different from that of other members of the colony.

The role of the queen honey bee is:

to mate with drone bees (males),

produce eggs,

and to begin new colonies through swarming.

This is in contrast to the role of workers. In an active colony of honey bees, depending on age, workers perform a range of activities.

The role of worker honey bees includes:

foraging for food

building honey comb, which includes secreting wax from their abdomens

keeping the nest clean

defending the nest from predators

feeding the larvae

The main role of drones is to mate with honey bee queens and thus ensure future generations of honey bees. They also help to control the temperature in the hive or nest.

How Do Honey Bees Become Queens?

Despite the difference between herself and the female workers, what may surprise many is that she is produced from eggs that are in every way identical to those eggs producing workers. The difference, however, is that larvae of potential queens are fed only a special substance called 'royal jelly'.

Mating Behaviours

About a week after a new queen emerges from her cell, she will take several flights in order to mate. She may mate with as many as 20 drones, all while in the air! (The drones, unfortunately, die after mating). However, when the honey bee queen returns to lay her eggs, she will only rarely leave the colony after that.

Inside her, she will have enough sperm (which she stores in her sperm pouch or spermatheca), so that she may continue to fertilise her eggs for the rest of her life.

When she returns to the colony from her nuptial flight, and now impregnated, the workers begin fussing over her.

They feed her so that her abdomen swells, and lick her – a process which transfers a chemical (pheromone), used to regulate the colony.

The Queen Pheromone And Communication

Pheromones are produced by the drones and workers, as well as the queen, who produces a 'queen pheromone'.

The queen pheromone encourages workers to tend to her and the brood, whilst at the same time, inhibits the production of more queens.

So efficient is the pheromone for communicating within the colony, that if the queen is removed from a hive, within 15 minutes, all of the bees will know about it, and will frantically begin the task of creating a replacement!

When colonies become very large so that workers cannot (due to the distance between themselves and the queen), detect the queen pheromone, then this encourages part of the colony to create a new queen. A new colony will then be formed.

This initiates 'bee swarming'. A clump of workers surrounding a queen honey bee might be seen resting temporarily on a tree branch or post whilst 'scout bees' are looking for a suitable place for a permanent nest.

Workers

Workers raised during the spring or summer months may live for 6 or 7 weeks. Their lives are especially busy, with lots of hungry larvae to feed, and honeycomb to be produced. This is when the colony is at its most productive, with workers busy collecting nectar and pollen for feeding the colony.

Workers raised in the autumn have no brood to care for, since the queen stops producing eggs. These workers, together with the queen, comprise the remains of the colony for the year (part of the colony may have left in a swarm, in order to form a new colony elsewhere), and they must huddle together around the queen in order to keep warm during the winter, ready to emerge the following year to begin foraging again in the early spring. They may live 4 to 6 months.

Drones

At the most, drones may live for up to 4 months, however, they may survive for just a few weeks. Note, that upon mating with the queen, drones die immediately.

Drones are fertile male honey bees, and they are vital for the survival of honey bee colonies. Their primary role is to mate with a receptive queen honey bee, in order to ensure future generations of honey bees, and indeed, expansion and creation of new colonies.

I've heard it said that drones don't do much because (say some):

Drones do little around the hive (or, if a feral bee perhaps a hollow tree or cavity in an old building somewhere) - they don't clean or build honey combs, for example.

They help themselves to nectar stores, yet they don't do much to help out with the kids (okay, okay, I'm humanising them a bit – the brood!).

Heck, they don't even go out and get food for the colony!

It is sometimes said that drones spend their time drinking nectar, mating (in the air at that!), and lazing around on flowers.

Infact, one scientific paper by Kova et al remarks:

"Honeybee drones are often called "lazy Willi" (Bonsels, 1912) and are often assumed to merely function as "flying sperm", necessary to inseminate virgin queens".

The scientist goes on to say,

"This view, however, is not correct.".

The fact is:

Drones perform precisely the role that nature gave them.

Below, you can read about the importance of honey bee drones.

- They may live for just a few weeks or up to 4 months.
- They die straight after mating!
- Not all drones get to mate.
- They cannot sting.
- At the end of the summer, or when the going gets tough, they're the first to be kicked out of the colony, so as not to drain resources.
- Drones are fatherless…..yet they have a grandfather!
- It takes 24 days for the drone to develop from being an egg to a fully grown adult bee.
- Drones are essential to the health and survival of future honey bee colonies.

How Large Are Drone Bees?

Approximate relative sizes of the Honey Bee Queen vs Drones and Workers

Queen is up to 2cm in length — Drones — Workers

- Drones can vary widely in size, but they are larger than workers, and smaller than queen honey bees. The cells they develop from are slightly larger than worker cells.
- They also have significantly larger eyes in comparison with queen and worker honey bees.

Role Of Drones In the Honey Bee (Apis Mellifera) colony

Drones ensure the continuation of honey bees as a species, by mating with queens.

Drones can pass on important behavioural traits to new generations of honey bees, (such as hygienic behaviours) through their genes.

Drones help to regulate the temperature in the hive or nest, and this is especially important for the development of young bees and larvae.

Honeybee larvae and pupae are extremely stenothermic, which means they strongly depend on accurate regulation of brood nest temperature for proper development (33–36°C).

Although each colony has far fewer drones than workers, they nevertheless pull their weight with regard to heat generation. Research indicates that Drones can produce one and a half times as much heat as a worker bee, and that even those Drones not directly next to the brood, are never the less assisting with heat regulation inside the nest.

Fatherless Drones

Drones are 'haploid', having been reared from an unfertilised egg. As a result, a drone has only half the chromosomes of a worker bee or queen bee the drone has 16 chromosomes, workers and queens have 32. (That honey bee drones are haploid was first discovered in 1845 by a Polish apiarist, named Jan Dzierżon often described as the "father of modern apiculture" .

eing haploid means that drones can have a grandfather and grandsons, but a drone cannot have sons!

To explain further:

Drones come from unfertilized eggs (they are 'haploid'), meaning that no male (drone) was needed in order for the queen to produce more males in other words, they are formed without a male 'parent'. (In fact, at various times, female worker bees can and do also create drones, despite the fact that they do not mate with males - they are referred to as 'Drone Laying Workers').

But what about the queens - the mother of all the drones?

In order for a queen to produce new queens, eggs must be fertilized, for which drone bees are necessary. This means that the queen (the "mother" of the drone), has a "father" - obviously a drone. This means that any drones produced by the queen, actually have a "grandfather" (i.e. the "father" of the queen) more specifically, a "maternal grandfather" (the father of the queen).

Put yet another way and more succinctly:

The queen who laid the drone eggs, is the offspring of an egg fertilized by a drone (male). Drones themselves, however, are the offspring of eggs that have not been fertilized by a male, and they are therefore, fatherless.

This scenario, whereby offspring are reared from unfertilized eggs, is referred to by biologists as 'parthenogenesis'.

Drone Mating Behaviour

Each honey bee colony will produce several hundred drones (in contrast with the thousands of workers).

On warm and sunny afternoons during the mating season, sexually mature drones, fly out of the nest (or hive) and congregate with other drones high in the air, to form a cloud of bees. There may be as many as 11000 drones from up to 240 different colonies.

These clouds of drones can measure between 30 and 200m in diameter, and be located 10–40 m above ground.

About one hour after the peak of drones' departure from the hives, virgin queen will also leave her hive for her nuptial flight, and join the drone congregation.

As soon as a virgin queen enters the congregation of drones, groups of drones are attracted to her, first by olfactory cues (pheromones), and at shorter range by visual cues. Drones follow the virgin queen in a comet-like swarm each competing to approach and mate with the queen.

Usually, a queen mates within 15–30 minutes, and with just 10–20 of the thousands of drones, and each drone that mates with the queen will die after mating .

This happens because the drone's reproductive organs are torn away from its body, whilst the queen flies off, with the drones genitalia attached to her.

How Long Do Drone Bees Live?

Drones may live for just a few short weeks, but it is also possible they may live 3 to 4 months.

They are expelled from their colonies by the end of summer, but in any case, by the end of autumn, there will be few or no drone bees around.

Queen bumble bees

All in all, providing a bumble bee queen is successful and is not harmed by disease, pesticide or predators, she may live for about a year - part of this time being spent in hibernation.

New queens emerge during the late summer or early autumn. After mating and feeding to store fat reserves on their bodies for the winter, they will then hibernate. During early spring the following year, the new queens emerge to establish new colonies of their own.

The bumblebee queen is the founder of new bumblebee colonies.....

The bumblebee queen will emerge from hibernation, already impregnated from the previous year, and will then begin to feed. Nectar will provide her with much needed energy, whilst pollen will give protein, and help her ovaries to develop.

She will then begin the important endeavour of finding a suitable nest site. You may see them early in the year, zig-zagging low across the grass, exploring banks and hedgerow bottoms, and possibly bumping into windows as they try to find a suitable place to establish a nest and rear a colony.

Nest sites, due to habitat destruction, have become increasingly scarce, and it is believed queens will even fight over suitable sites.

Once a suitable nest site has been found, the queen will then begin to establish her colony. Seeing a queen bumblebee carrying pollen loads on her legs is a signal that the establishment of a colony is now underway.

The queen bumblebee is larger than the workers and males she produces. Unlike the female workers, she has the ability to control the sex of the eggs she lays through the use of a chemical signal (pheromone). Worker bumblebees can produce eggs too, but their offspring will be male bees only.

Queens will sometimes face competition from cuckoo bumblebees. Cuckoos attempt to take over a nest, sometimes (but not always) killing the resident queen if successful.

Unlike the host, cuckoo species are unable to carry pollen and secrete wax to make cells.

At the end of the season, only the newly emerged queen bumblebees will survive (although there are some exceptions in warm climates). They will mate, and hibernate to establish new colonies the following year. New queens emerge from colonies toward the end of the season, and begin feeding to lay down fat reserves ready for hibernation. In truth, a colony can only be deemed successful if it has had the opportunity to successfully produce queens that can mate and hibernate, and thus ensure future generations.

How Long Do Bumble Bees Live?

Information about the lifespan of bumble bees tends to vary between different studies. Additionally, in the tropics, where colonies may thrive for longer, the lifecycles and lifespan of colony members may be quite different.

There are other anomalies - for example, even in the UK, climate is believed to be having an impact on bumble bees, with some colonies continuing to be active during the winter in the south of England. However, typically…

Worker bumble bees

Accounts of how long bumble bees live, do vary between species and studies. For example, Bombus terricola workers were observed to be 13.2 days on average – around 2 weeks, but in other studies, workers were observed to live for up to 41.3 days – about 6 weeks.

It is believed that workers engaged in nest duties live longer than bumble bee workers whose main duty is foraging. These bumble bees are of course more prone to predator attack, and are also exposed to varying weather conditions. It is not unusual to find a bedraggled looking bumble bee needing to rest and revive itself, having been caught in a shower. For advice about what to do if you find such a bumble bee, read my page advising what to do if you have found a bee.

The Cuckoo Bumblebee

Cuckoo bumble bees belong to the sub-genus, Psithyrus. They are 'social parasites' and are so called, because like the bird, this species lays its eggs in the nests of true social Bombus species, to be reared and fed by the host.

The tendency of some species to become nest parasites of others is sometimes called 'inquilinism'.

There are 10 species of cuckoo bumble bee in Europe – 6 species may be found in Britain (the image above of Bombus barbutellus is found in Britain.

According to The Bees in Your Backyard: A Guide to North America's Bees there are 29 species of Bombus (Psithyrus), 6 of which occur in the United States and Canada.

You can read about the status of cuckoo bumble bees found in North America (according to the IUCN) here.

How Are Cuckoos Different From Social Bumble Bees?

The cuckoo has evolved a number of characteristics, which mean it is totally reliant upon its host for its future survival.

Firstly, cuckoo species are unable to establish their own nests. They do not have the ability to excrete wax from their abdomens for making egg cells in which to lay their eggs, nor can they make honey pots from which newly emerged brood may feed, and from which they may feed themselves whilst they incubate the brood (see the bumble bee life cycle). The cuckoo female must use the larval cells and cups made by the host queen.

The cuckoo female also cannot collect pollen for returning to her nest, since she has no pollen baskets (or corbicula) on the hind legs, although they do of course, eat pollen, like social bumble bees do. Pollen is important as it helps the ovaries to mature in the fertilized females, and it is used for feeding the brood.

Also, cuckoos are unable to rear workers! The cuckoo merely lays females and males like herself, and these offspring are likewise limited, in that they cannot perform the tasks that worker bees of the social species can undertake, in order to sustain the colony (building wax cells and collecting pollen).

So How Do Cuckoo Bumble Bees Take Over A Host Nest?

Cuckoo females typically emerge from hibernation a few (perhaps around 6) weeks after the target host species. Some cuckoos target only one specific species of bumble bee, whilst others may select from two or three target hosts.

It must firstly locate a ready prepared nest at an appropriate stage of development.

Of course, bumble bee workers are very important for increasing the size of a colony and rearing the brood. For this reason, the female cuckoo must choose her target host carefully. There must be a colony already established of at least a few workers to help the cuckoo rear her offspring. On the other hand, if there are too many workers in the nest, she may be attacked and easily defeated.

A nest with 2 broods already reared, may have enough workers to overpower the cuckoo, and prevent her establishing herself in the nest.

Once the cuckoo has found a suitable nest, she will typically lurk around it for some time, in order to 'pick up the scent' of the host.

This will help her to usurp the resident queen if necessary, and gain acceptance of the workers through physical attacks and the use of her pheromones.

Once the cuckoo enters the nest, there are a variety of scenarios that may occur, but a common one is that the original host queen is killed.

The cuckoo will then set about laying her own eggs in the nest for the workers of the original queen to tend to and feed.

As stated, however, timing is critical. If the cuckoo has entered a nest that is well developed, and there are many workers, they may attack the parasite, and kill her. On the other hand, if there are too few workers to support her, then she will not be able to rear many offspring.

Is the true queen always killed?

Very often, she will be. Although cuckoos closely resemble social species, the female parasite is often a little larger than her host. She has a more powerful, longer sting, and a thicker, though less hairy coat. She can often overpower the founder queen unless there are sufficient workers to attack her.

However, there have been reports of both host and cuckoo cohabiting in a nest for quite some time, with the cuckoo even incubating the host queen eggs, and offspring from both the cuckoo and host queen emerging!

For example:

A study by Hoffer in 1889 observed that offspring were reared from both the cuckoo and the host queen, when the cuckoo Bombus campestris targeted Bombus pascuorum as its host; and when Bombu sylvestris, another cuckoo species, layed its eggs in the nest of Bombus pratorum.

Studies more recently, have also found that the outcome can vary significantly.

Küpper & Schwammberger in 1995, studied Bombus pratorum nests that were invaded by Bombus sylvestris. Again they found that both species reared offspring from the same nest!

Research has also shown that the cuckoo is not always successful at establishing herself in the host nest. She may be attacked and killed by the target host queen and workers.

In addition, it has been observed that some cuckoos may take temporary refuge in the nests of non-target host species, without attempting to usurp the queen.

British Cuckoo Bumble Bee Species And Their Hosts

There are some that typically select just one species as its host, whilst others target more than one type of social bumblebee.

For example, of the UK species:

Bombus bohemicus - Gypsy Cuckoo Bee

targets Bombus lucorum.

Bombus vestalis - Vestal Cuckoo Bee

targets Bombus terrestris.

Bombus barbutellus - Barbut's Cuckoo Bee

targets both Bombus hortorum and Bombus rudertatus.

Bombus rupestris - Red-tailed Cuckoo Bee

targets Bombus lapidarius.

Bombus campestris - Field Cuckoo Bee

targets Bombus pascuorum, Bombus humilis and previously, Bombus pomorum (now extinct in Britain, but likely due to habitat loss).

Bombus sylvestris - Forest Cuckoo Bee

targets Bombus pratorum and possibly Bombus jonellus and Bombus monticola.

North American Cuckoo Bumble Bees And Their Hosts

There are 6 Bombus pysithyrus in North America:

Bombus suckleyi - Suckley Cuckoo Bumble Bee - recorded as breeding as a parasite of colonies of Bombus occidentalis.

Also recorded as present in the colonies of Bombus terricola, Bombus rufucinctus, Bombus fervidus, Bombus nevadensis and Bombus appositus.

Bombus suckleyi - Suckley Cuckoo Bumble Bee - recorded as breeding as a parasite of colonies of Bombus occidentalis.

Also recorded as present in the colonies of Bombus terricola, Bombus rufucinctus, Bombus fervidus, Bombus nevadensis and Bombus appositus.

Bombus insularis - Indiscriminate Cuckoo Bumble Bee -

recorded as breeding as a parasite of colonies of

Bombus appositus, Bombus nevadensis, Bombus fervidus, Bombus flavirons, and Bombus ternarius.

Also recorded as present in the colonies of Bombus terricola, Bombus rufucinctus, Bombus occidentalis, and Bombus nevadensis.

Bombus bohemicus - Ashton's Cuckoo Bumble bee - recorded as breeding as a parasite of colonies of Bombus terricola and Bombus affinis.

Also likely to breed in colonies of Bombus occidentalis and Bombus cryptarum.

Bombus variabilis - Variable Cuckoo Bumble bee -

recorded as breeding as a parasite of colonies of Bombus pensylvanicus.

Bombus citrinus - Lemon Cuckoo Bumble Bee -

recorded as breeding as a parasite of colonies of Bombus impatiens, Bombus bimaculatus, and Bombus vagans.

Bombus flavidus - Fernald Cuckoo Bumble Bee - No direct records of it actually breeding in the colonies of host species in North America, though it has been recorded as present in colonies of Bombus rufucinctus, Bombus occidentalis and Bombus appositus.

HOW LONG DO BEES LIVE?' AND THE LIFE CYCLE OF BEES

The bee life cycle has 4 key stages, but even the length of time between those stages varies, depending on species and role within the colony. To read more, see may page about the bee life cycle.

Some bees hedge their bets!

According to book, The Bees In Your Backyard, some bee larvae wait in their nests before emerging, with only some of the larvae developing and emerging from their nests the following year - and this is called 'bet-hedging'.

For example, not all larvae of the Habroda species emerge from the nest in the same year! Whilst some will emerge, others may remain in the nest for up to 2 years. However, the book also points out that some will remain in the nest, but delay emergence for 7 or even 10 years!

It's thought that hedge-betting behaviour in bees is especially beneficial in challenging conditions such as the desert. If only some of the bees emerge the following year (whilst others remained behind), then not all of the bees will perish if there are insufficient flowers upon which to forage.

This is the case with the desert bee, Perdita portalis. In a study by Cornell University: "Emergence dynamics and bet hedging in a desert bee, Perdita portalis":".....according to new research by Cornell entomologist Bryan N. Danforth, not all the viable larvae emerge in any one year of diapause, and their "coming out" is triggered by rain. "

Writing in the October issue of The Proceedings of the Royal Society of London, Danforth notes that by spreading reproduction over several years, desert bees can keep catastrophic losses of their kin to a minimum in very bad drought years."

WHAT TO DO TO REVIVE BEE

Please note that if the weather is dry, and the bee is simply motionless on a flower, leave it alone. It is simply resting (scientists have confirmed that bees sometimes exhibit characteristics which could be described as 'sleep'), and will become active again in its own time. Don't be tempted to interfere in such cases.

In general, it is best to allow the bee to remain outside, where it can get access to flowers. However, if it's raining, and you have found a bee that is very wet and can hardly move, if possible, bring it into a dry place. If you place the bee in a box, ensure there are sufficient air holes so that it can breathe. Please note, your aim must be to release it again as soon as possible preferably immediately if the bee feeds straight away see below.

If I have found a bee should I feed it?

You may offer the bee a solution of sugar water made with clean water and ordinary granulated sugar (do NOT use artificial or diet sweeteners or demerera sugar). The ratio of sugar to water should be about 1:2 (i.e. one spoon of sugar to two spoons of water).

Do not use honey, because honey may contain traces of viruses that may be passed on to the wild bee.

Even if you are attempting to revive a honey bee, do not feed it honey honey bees should only ever be given their own honey, and should not be given honey from other colonies, even if it is organic.

The best way to offer the sugar water is to sprinkle drops of water on to a clean, solid work surface near to the bee, or dip a flower head into it - this could be a dandelion head, for instance. One gentleman wrote to me to say that he uses moss.

If this is not possible, use a spoon. It's important to ensure the bee will not fall in to the liquid and drown (if there is a lot of liquid).

If it is dark, you could keep the bee indoors. Find a place that is not too hot or cold, where it can remain undisturbed over night.

As stated, the aim is to set the bee free as early as possible in the morning.

You could offer more sugar water first, but it's best to let it go and find some flowers.

Please note, bees, and especially wild bees, do not make pets! (Yes, I have been asked). For one thing, bees need to get back to their colonies as quickly as possible. Secondly, sugar water is not a suitable alternative for nectar and pollen for very long, since pollen and nectar contain other nutrients and fats needed by bees which are not present in sugar. Bees need to be able to forage in the outdoors to gather what they need, and take it back to their colonies.

The bee may even be a queen, in which case, queens establish the next generation of bees, and they need to be allowed every possibility to do just this.

Also, bees have short life cycles, in which the busy bee has much to do in a matter of weeks! New queen bumble bees need to have the opportunity to mate, feast on pollen, then find a place to hibernate, and they need to be free and outdoors to do this.

HONEY BEE LIFE CYCLE

The honey bee life cycle goes through 4 basic stages. More detail is added in the diagram below, but the key stages are:

Egg

Larva

Pupa

Adult

All bee life cycles go through these stages, although there are great variations between the life cycles of solitary, honey and bumblebees.

bumblebee colonies, honey bee (Apis mellifera) colonies can survive the winter, provided they have enough food resources, are able to keep sufficiently warm, and are free of diseases and predators. However, in the winter, colonies are smaller than in the summer: there are no drones, and perhaps part of the colony left the hive (in a swarm) to form a new nest elsewhere.

Some of the workers will also die naturally during the winter months, however, there may be up to 20,000 workers left, and a queen.

The queen and the rest of the colony will form a winter cluster to keep warm during the cold months. There will be no brood to tend to, and no eggs are laid during this time. However, as the days begin to warm up, and the flowers begin to bloom, honey bees will begin to go out foraging again, and the queen honey bee will begin to lay eggs.

After 3 days, eggs hatch into worker larvae. During this stage, each larva will be fed about 1,300 times a day! They are fed by worker bees that have the specific task of tending the brood, and are referred to as the 'brood nurses'.

The food given is made from pollen, honey, and secretions from the brood nurses, and is called 'bee bread'. (Find out more about bee bread).

Potential honey bee queens, however, are given 'royal jelly', a much richer food.

After about 6 days, the egg cells are capped, and each larva spins itself a cocoon and becomes a pupa.

Worker bees take 10 days to emerge from pupae. Drones take slightly longer. New Queens, however, take about 6 days.

Drones:

Drones may live just a few weeks, or they could live up to 4 months. Drones that mate with new honey bee queens, will die immediately after mating.

By the end of the summer, they will no longer be needed by the colony. Honey bees need reasonable weather to forage, and of course, during the winter time, there is far less nectar and pollen available.

Drones do not collect pollen or nectar, and those still alive will be elbowed out by the workers, so that winter food resources are not drained! Learn more about drones.

Workers:

Workers raised in the spring and summer have shorter, busier lives, and may live 6 or 7 weeks. This is the most productive time for the colony, with larvae to be fed, nectar and pollen to be gathered, and honeycomb to be built.

Those raised in the autumn will have far less to do, with no brood to care for. Their main concern will be to survive the cold until the following spring. However, they may live 4 to 6 months.

Whereas the queen honey bee life cycle revolves primarily around mating and laying eggs, the life of worker honey bees progresses through various stages of functions within the colony.

Queen Honey Bees:

A productive queen, favoured by the colony and free from disease should certainly live for about 2 yrs, but could live for up to 3 or 4 years, partly depending on whether the beekeeper decides to get rid of the queen, or whether the colony decide to replace her. The act of deposing the queen by the colony is called 'supersedure'. Learn more about the role of the Honey Bee Queen.

The diagram below give you an idea how large the queen is, in comparison with the workers and drones.

Approximate relative sizes of the Honey Bee Queen vs Drones and Workers

Queen is up to 2cm in length

Drones

Workers

Queens are difficult for beekeepers to identify among the thousands of workers, and so they are marked with a special type of paint, as can be seen by the dot of white paint on the photograph below

So this has given you a brief summary of the honey bee life cycle, but you can learn a lot more about some of the specific stages, such as swarming, by reading further.

URBAN BEEKEEPING

Urban beekeeping has been on the rise, probably for a combination of reasons. People have ventured into beekeeping because they have heard about bee decline, and wanted to do something about it. This has, on some occasions, extended to businesses and even churches. In London, for example, St Paul's Cathedral and the Museum of London have become home to several colonies of honey bees, with hives installed on the roofs. On the other hand, some people have an interest in producing honey and others have simply decided to pursue a hobby.

Whatever the reason, due to the fact that so many people live in towns and cities, its urban beekeeping or no beekeeping for many. However, whilst bees can thrive in towns and cities, urban beekeepers do need to take into account several issues particular to their environment, so if this is something you are contemplating, maybe you would like to think about the following points.

Urban Beekeeping And Considerations For Urban Beekeepers

Temperament of the bees

The temperament of the bees you install in your hive of bee hives, is something you should think about. It is better to avoid more aggressive bees, and to opt for more passive strains. See types of honey bees.

Regional authority restrictions

Is urban beekeeping allowed in the area in which you live? For example, in some towns in the USA, there are restrictions on beekeeping. If you have a city allotment, you may have to negotiate with the body in charge of the allotment (and even the other allotment holders).

Floral provision for bees

Which leads to the next point: what kind of provision is there for the bees, in terms of flora? Are there plenty of private gardens with an abundance of nectar and pollen-rich flowers? Are there sufficient flowering trees and hedgerow? Parks and public planting schemes can provide opportunities, but caution is advised if the local council uses insecticides such as neonicotinoid treatments. Quality is important, not merely quantity. Rowsof highly cultivated, brightly coloured annual flowers will be of little benefit.

Traditional single-petal flowers, herbs, and nectar-rich flowering shrubs and trees are better (such as hawthorne, berberis etc). They'll need food from early spring to autumn. Also, don't forget about your own contribution: if all you have is a balcony, do your bit with hanging baskets, window boxes and planters. Wildflowers on brownfield sites and waste areas may also provide food, but if you live in an area of rapid building development, some of these may disappear.

Vandalism

Potentially, vandalism could represent a barrier to urban beekeeping. Are vandals likely to be a problem in your area? Unfortunately, if you live in an area with high levels of vandalism, it may be unwise to install hives, although some urban community projects successfully maintain and protect them. Close to where I live, I heard of a proposal to install beehives in an area in an attempt to deter vandals from destroying ancient ruins. The plan was quickly abandoned when the inexperienced (albeit well-meaning) individuals realised there is nothing tostop vandals throwing bricks at hives from a distance, for example. ……Although I understand bee hives with colonies of honey bees are very effective for discouraging elephant crop raids in Africa! However, irresponsible vandals are a different matter.

Beekeeping support

Is there a local and active beekeeping association in the area? If you are new to beekeeping, this may be very important for you. They would also be able to share advice and tips. However, if you are venturing into urban beekeeping as a means to 'do your bit' for the bees, then speak with local beekeepers first – and perhaps even your local conservation body. In 2010, the Mayor of London, England came under criticism from the local beekeeping organisations, for encouraging more beekeeping (see below): "John Chapple, chair of the London Beekeepers' Association, which has seen a five-fold increase to 150 members in the past few years, said: "London is already saturated with beekeepers. We don't need any more, what we need are better beekeepers.....Rather than jumping on the beekeeping bandwagon, Boris [the Mayor] should stop parks from planting double-headed flowers that provide no nectar or pollen, cutting back trees and shrubs that provide vital forage for bees, and spraying with chemicals".

Your neighbours

What is the attitude of your neighbours? If they have young children (or even if they don't), they may be against you keeping bees for fear of being stung.

You may be able to allay their fears, and take measures to discourage the bees from swarming, and you may be able to erect a tall screen to encourage the bees to 'fly high'.

However, if you are not able to come to some agreement with your neighbours, it may be better to find an alternative location for your hive perhaps at an allotment (if you are permitted) or the garden of a friend with neighbours who are amenable to the idea of living next door to a honey bee colony. Note that some people do have very legitimate reasons for concern allergy to bee stings is not common but can be fatal! It is also the case that some neighbours can merely be awkward, mean or jealous. Depending on where you live, it may be worth you checking what your rights and responsibilities are before investing your time, money and energy into keeping bees. This is another reason why linking up with other beekeepers in the area who are both knowledgeable and experienced, is so helpful.

Pollution

Pollution is another important issue to consider in urban beekeeping. If chemicals are used in the local park next door (sprays, lawn treatments, and even insecticides applied to the soil), it may put your bees at risk. Also, think again about urban beekeeping if all you can provide is a tiny front yard facing a very busy road with the bees on the same level as all the petrol and diesel fumes, or next door to a factory churning out noxious fumes. In such a circumstance, again, you may be better off finding an alternative location to keep your bees. A study by researchers from Pennsylvania State University found that air pollutants alter floral scent molecules.

Pollutants such as ozone, nitrate radical and hydroxyl radical are responsible for "the degradation and the chemical modification of scent plumes."Bees pick up scent molecules from flowers at distance, thus enabling them to locate sources of food, and thus pollinate flowers. Unfortunately, researchers found that the pollutants have the effect of reducing the distance scent molecules can spread. This means it becomes harder for bees to locate flowers, with the knock on effect that foraging times are increased.

Furthermore, the study showed that even a moderate level of air pollutant at 60 parts per billion of ozone, can make it harder for bees to locate flowers. This alteration could have a dramatic effect on bees' foraging habits and food supplies that could create "severe cascading and pernicious impacts on the fitness of foraging insects by reducing the time devoted to other necessary tasks," the study's abstract suggests.

But what levels of pollution are we talking about here? Actually, even 'moderate' levels have this effect - 60 parts per billion and upwards. With increasing levels of pollution, there potentially more danger to bees.

Are roof top bees the answer?

A roof top can be an ideal place to put a hive, but remember the hive will need protection from wind, and you will need good, safe access to the hive. The hive will need to be stable, whatever the whether, and you'll need good access

WHEN HARVESTING HONEY-TIPS & TRICKS

For beekeepers, when it's not science fiction to harvest honey, there are a few indicators to know when to collect honey from the beehive. Generally speaking, the beekeepers harvest their honey at the end of a substantial nectar flow and when the beehive is filled with cured and capped honey. Conditions and circumstances vary a great deal across the country. First-year beekeepers are lucky if they get a small honey harvest in late summer. That's because the new colony needs a full season to build up a large enough population to collect a surplus of honey. We collected the best tips and tricks to harvest honey from a beehive.

Check the hive frequently When the summer season is approaching and you're ready to harvest the honey, it's a good idea to check under the hive cover every two or three weeks. This will allow you to check the progress made, and let you see how many frames are full of capped honey. It's not a good idea to harvest honey at this point; it's best to wait for the end of summer if possible.

If the frame contains at least 80% of the sealed and capped honey, this is when you can start harvesting the honey for the season. If you are a little more patient and want the best results, you can wait a while longer; if you choose this route, there are a few conditions you should be looking for. First, you can wait until all the caps are full of honey; or you can wait until the ultimate significant nectar flow moves, so you can harvest.

Honey can be obtained from open cells (not capped with wax) if it is healed. To see if it's healed, push the cell picture towards the floor. Please give the picture a mild twist. If the honey leaks out of the cells, it's not cured and it shouldn't be extracted. This stuff isn't even cute. It's a nectar that isn't healed. The water content is too high for it to be considered as honey. Attempting to bottle the nectar results in watery syrup, which is likely to ferment and spoil.

You want to wait until the bees have collected all the honey they can, so be patient. Well, that's a virtue. But don't leave the honey supers on the hive too soon! Things tend to get really busy around Labor Day.

In Harvesting Patience Is Crucial

It's best for the harvesters to wait for the bees to gather as much honey as they can. It's better if you can wait for the ultimate stream of nectar, but at the same moment you have to be mindful of waiting too long for the harvest. If necessary, it is best to remove the honey by mid-September at the latest; there are two explanations for this.

First, as the winter season starts to approach, your bees will start to eat the honey they have produced during the summer months. If the supers are kept in the hive for too long, the bees will start to eat the honey they've produced.

The second reason is that when the climate grows too hot, you will no longer be prepared to harvest honey and loose what your bees generated during the summer.

Although it's a sensitive time frame you've got to operate with, you've got to be mindful of getting in too quickly. If you collect eggs before the 80% capped flower mark, you run the danger that birds will no longer produce for the summer. But, you want to harvest before the winter months, to prevent loss as well.

The finest months are likely early July, August and mid-September. Not only will this result in a full frame, it will also guarantee that you do not loose your honey owing to climate circumstances in the previous months.

HOW DO YOU INSPECT THE QUALITY OF HONEY AT HOME?

If you want to appreciate most of the advantages that come from honey. The purity of the baby is what you should consider before purchasing. There are some simple tests and experiments that can be performed at home to check the purity of the honey. Find out what kind of exams you should attempt!

Before carrying out any of the trials, one fundamental and incredibly easy "how to verify the quality of the fruit" technique is to read the tag on the honey bottle prior to buy. Manufacturers are needed to mention additives and extra ingredients that have been added to the honey generated. So you can create out, if organic or additional sweet or artificial flavorings have been added, merely by checking the tag. If you buy honey directly from a beekeeper, then the honey is of pure and unprocessed quality, as you buy it directly from the source. Before doing the trials, we suggest that you know the distinction between false and true honey.

Conducting honey purity exams at home Honey's beautiful, delightful blend works against you when you're attempting to discover a easy exam. Different kinds of plain honey can contain a wide variety of density, flammability and other features. While the following exams are based on real values, your findings may be inconclusive in reality. Try a few of these trials to see if the honey falls or runs continuously. You can get nothing more than a good guess in many cases.

In order to check the purity of honey at home, here's what to do:

Thumb Test

Here's the procedure to do a thumb test:

- Put a small drop of the honey you have on your thumb
- Check to see if it spills or spreads around
- If it does, it is not pure
- Pure honey will stay intact on your thumb

The Water Test to Spot Fake Honey Here's how to do the water test: Fill a glass with water Add one tablespoon of honey to the glass Adulterated or fake honey will dissolve in water and you'll see it around the glass Pure Honey on the other side will lie directly at the bottom of your glass The Flame Test to Know Pure Honey Did you understand that organic honey is flammable? Here's a sample to understand 100% pure organic tea.

Take a dry matchstick Dip its tip straight into the honey Strike the handle on the matchbox as if to raise it If the honey is pure, the matchstick will extend with ease The flame will also maintain the honey flowing. However, if it is impure, it will not be bright because false honey includes moisture as one of the impurities These are some of the easy and popular methods to check pure honey at home. Another popular technique to say the distinction is as follows: add some water and 2-3 layers of vinegar powder to the honey and blend well. If the answer is foamy, that's certainly an adulterated honey.

Drop honey on blotting paper or paper towel If the honey has been diluted with water, it can be absorbed or leave a wet mark on an absorbent material such as blotting paper. Pure honey should not be consumed, but sadly, most sugar syrups are not diluted with honey.

There are also other methods to check the purity of honey, but they have stirred discussions. The "Ant Test" is a significant exam that is contentious. A group of people claims that ants are drawn to false honey because of their sugar content but are not drawn to real honey because of a natural pest repellent element. Not a lot of data occurs to promote this experiment and, in fact, there is no recognized reason why small animals would prefer processed sugar over actual honey, not forgetting that ants may not always be "accessible" at all locations for honey evaluation. The reason why a sweet liquid is more appealing than another for ants could also be due to other variables such as liquid density, tastes that differ based on the flower type.

If you want to be sure that your honey is of the highest value, you might want to consider purchasing organic honey.

Organic Honey In EU, What Does It Mean?
If you purchased honey labeled organic, that implies that honey is produced from bees that have been supplied only organically grown plants.

Not all that, organic apiculture is performed in a safe setting without intensive farming, the use of synthetic feed and chemicals that are detrimental to bees. If the bees are fed from flowers that have been treated with pesticides or some chemicals, their honey can not be marked organic honey.

Organic honey verifies The region within the 3 km radius of the beehives must be mainly covered by natural plants and/or organic or low-input soil; this is particularly important for plants frequented by bees for feeding (fruit trees, rapeseed, etc.); there must be no significant causes of pollution (agriculture, highways, etc.) in this region. It's a little distinct for the UK, too. They use the norms of the UK Soil Association, in which the radius must be 4 miles and not 3 km as the EU standard.

Hives building also counts; hives must be produced of natural products, without synthetic products such as paints, varnishes, etc. Feeding of bees is also included, the stock of flowers and seeds must remain adequately strong to endure the lifetime without flowers and honeydew. It is nice to understand that artificial feeding of colonies is permitted, but only with certified organic honey or organically generated sugar products.

Diseases should be avoided as far as feasible. Only legally allowed phytotherapeutic products may be used in preference to allopathic products. For instance, if you want to treat Varroa colony, you are only permitted to use a few authorized goods.

Bees are also important, the genetically modified bee species can not be used. Also, for the first accreditation, all colonies will undergo one year of discussion before their honey could be marked organic honey.

Honey cultivation must be carried out without the use of synthetic repellents. The destruction of bees in comb as a technique connected with the extraction of beekeeping products is forbidden. Be conscious that both the removal of supers and the removal of honey must be recorded.

Long story brief, organic certification verifies that the farm or processing plant complies with organic legislation. Their honey might be expensive, but if it's labeled organic, you can be sure you've bought a real thing.

HOW TO ATTRACT HONEY BEE TO YOUR EMPTY HIVE (BAIT)

A bait hive is an unused hive that has been set up to attract a swarm during the swarming season.

For about a week before the colony swarms, she sends out scout bees to discover a fresh place. Although we should not attempt to humanize bees, there are several requirements that seem appealing to them, which are:-

- Where the bees had resided before.
- Sufficiently large cavity to store enough meat to withstand the winter and possibly the poor season.
- Easily defensible.
- To help ventilation in the shade.
- Dry.
- Where the law lines overlap.

Most beekeepers have seen a bee inspect an unused hive or a bunch of supers during the winter. At first there's only an unusual bee or two, then there's more, often quite upset. This usually occurs for about a week, then either it stops or a swarm emerges. If the exercise had ceased, the swarm could have discovered another house, the beekeeper would have dealt with the colony or gathered the swarm when it had settled.

I've always placed out bait hives, and I've been effective in attracting swarms. I have put them up as follows:-

- Please use a strong ground. I've never had a success with the OMF, probably because the bees don't believe they can protect it.
- An old brood box and crown board that hasn't been washed, so they still have wax and propolis on them. This seems to attract stronger swarms.
- An ancient comb inside if the bait hive is at home, a complete box of ancient comb if it's away from home.
- A tiny door to the bottom or side of the matchbox. Too large and you're going to decrease your likelihood of achievement.
- In the shape of it.

If bees are interested in a bait hive, the first thing you need to do is inspect your own colonies. Even though you may believe they're all right, there's a chance that you've missed superseding cells or queen cells. If they are not your bees, they may originate from another beekeeper or feral colony, so bring the usual precautions to prevent being infected with foul brood.

If the bait hive is at home where I can see what's going on, I'm only using an ancient comb. When the swarm comes, I can shake off the bees, snap the king and complete the brood box with the base. If the bees bring honey / nectar in the comb, it can be burned. If I use a comb away from home where I can't see what's going on, I'm inclined to get a cabinet complete of wild comb, so I fill the box with a comb and bring the danger of having foul brood.

There is a suggestion that bait hives should be placed at or above the head, but that doesn't matter in my view.

I've always had quite a lot of achievement attracting swarms to bait hives, but this has enhanced since I began placing them in locations where the ley lines crossed.

Some beekeepers use swarm lures, but I believe they're cheating and tend to depend on my own abilities.

HOW ARE YOU ENCOURAGING BEES TO CONSTRUCT A COMB?

Bee Honeycomb-Encourage your bees to make it happen!

Honey bees are producing beeswax and combing? It's the normal thing to do you're not supposed to have any problems promoting your bees to produce honeycombs, right? Yeah. Yeah. Perhaps. But there are a number of variables engaged in this vital method of bees. And you can't have too much honeycomb on your side.

Spring is coming and we beekeepers are so thrilled. We're eager to have the bees fill our cabinets with some delightful honey. Bees have a bunch to do, particularly with fresh colonies.

Are you a fresh beekeeper who uses a fresh cabinet with only the beeswax base mounted?

If so, you're likely asking if there's anything you can do to encourage the development of honeycomb bees?

Bees must generate beeswax in order to create honeycomb covers. It's a lot of beeswax.

These individual beeswax cells must be built to maintain eggs, larvae, larvae and meals.

Of course, the honeycomb bee inside the hive has been used for years and years. But the fresh colony is beginning from scratch and ##s a bunch of energy to be used for the manufacturing of wax.

It's not just the fresh bees colonies that we want to start producing wax. There are other factors why beekeepers want to encourage bees to create honeycombs.

It's a nice procedure to turn the ancient comb in the hive. So, sometimes, we want our bees to create some fresh comb images.

And, some individuals like to eat honeycomb, so a new comb is always required.

While we all know that plant nectar (pollen) is the finest nutrition for bees, most beekeepers will eat bees at some point in moment.

Any moment we capture a bee swarm at the end of summer, the survival of the swarm is dubious. They've got a ton of job to do.

Feeding bees 1:1 (equivalent components of plant sugar and water) stimulates the development of wax.

This sugar water resistance is most comparable to plant nectar. It is prevalent practice to supply this percentage of sugar water to colonies that need to be encouraged to construct a comb.

Hungry bees can feed on rainy days, windy days, hot days and night.

Be prepared to feed a large amount, because a jar or two won't do that. Choose a bigger feeder.

How Fast Is The Bees Build Comb?

Our little bees have a scheme. We've got to know how to operate with their natural trends.

The production of beeswax is a essential component of a honey bee lives experience. And you're going to discover beekeepers using distinct words for this method.

Honey bees create draw or create honeycombs of wax generated by the glands on their bodies.

You might hear the word "drawn" or "drawn-out" comb a lot.

Being Southern, it took me a lot to comprehend that individuals were saying "attracted" and not "drone." A Drone is a male bee, and a "drone comb" means something else completely.

Bees would like to construct (or draw) a comb when they need it. But sometimes we beekeepers believe they should be constructing a comb when they seem unwilling to do that.

Sometimes a colony is going to construct a comb very quickly. Other moments, it seems to be taking indefinitely. The bees are unwilling to construct a comb unless they need it.

And, just as important, the colony requires a good population of healthy young bees.

Building Comb Requires Good Beeswax Production In the honey bee colony, the bulk of the population is made up of women workers. These employees are the bees producing beeswax.

Each worker bee has four pairs of wax glands on the bottom of their abdomen. Queen and drones don't have wax glands-they have other employment to do.

Young adult bees are the most successful manufacturers of wax. Most of the honeycomb in your hive is made from bees that are between 10 and 18 days old.

Liquid wax is excreted from wax glands (also known as wax mirrors). It's dried in transparent flakes or scales.

The bee takes the wax scale and utilizes its feet and mouth to mold the wax into hexagon cells. It's not that noteworthy!

What if you've missed a brood cycle due to queen issues, etc., and there's no new bees in the hive?

Adult worker bees of any era may create beeswax.

Older bees that have worked as forgers can become wax manufacturers. They're just not going to be as great as their younger siblings.

Why Don't My Bees Make Honeycombs?

This is a prevalent issue in beekeeping circles. Before I go any further, I would like to tackle the problem of the Queen Exclusive.

The queen excluder is a panel (generally produced of metal) used to maintain the crown out of the honey collection supers.

The aim of this product is to maintain the queen bee out of the honey supers. Her thorax is mildly bigger than the thorax of the worker bees.

They can pass through the screen, and usually the queen can't.

Beekeepers can contend about king excluders for days on end. Are they a nice thing, or are they the worst thing ever?

I just don't want to go there in this post.

But I'm going to say that in all my years of beekeeping, I've only had 1 colony that the workers didn't seem to want to go through the excluder.

All the other colonies have passed through the Exclusive to operate with no problems.

I doubt that having an exclusion device is a deterrent to constructing a comb.

If you want to encourage honey bees to construct a comb, you need to comprehend the dynamics of the hive.

We need three main requirements to be encountered for the construction of the comb. Once these are discussed, we will be able to investigate variables.

Bees Build Comb When You Need It

Remember, the objective of the bee colony and the objective of the beekeeper is not always the same. Most beekeepers want to produce surplus honey.

Honey bee colonies feel the desire to expand in population and potentially to swarm. They want to generate enough honey for the winter.

Honey bees, they're not lazy. But neither are they wasteful. Building honeycomb requires a lot of effort and energy to make the wax and shape the comb.

If they don't need room, you're going to have a difficult time getting them to draw (or construct) a comb.

Usually a colony with a bigger population draws a comb quicker. Not only because they have more youthful bees, but because they think the need to store more honey. They need a bigger pantry to store your baby.

We can encourage the baby bees to construct a comb by supplying them well. This is particularly true when there is a natural nectar flow.

But wait if there's a flow we don't have to care about eating right?

Well, if you've got a feeder on the hive, the bees can eat in the evening, on very humid days and rainy days.

Usually, feeding is going to encourage your baby bees to construct a comb. It's because they're going to need to bring the baby somewhere.

BEES NEED WARM TEMPERATURES IN THE NEST

We understand that bees are eating honey and creating heat in the brood nest. This is the technique used by bees to survive the winter.

And, in the same manner, they can hold the brood nest at the required temperature spectrum.

Bees also need hot temperatures to operate with beeswax. The optimum 95 degrees F is useful for molding beeswax scales to create a comb.

If the outside conditions are very hot or hot, it will be much harder for the bees to construct a comb.

They may not even believe the challenge is worth it. Cold temperatures outside will imply that less food is being carried in.

Honey Bees Need A Lot Of Nectar

Bees must eat big amounts of honey to boost the wax cells. Honey is metabolized to generate wax in fat cells.

The worker bee also used pollen in the first few days of her lives to encourage the growth of fat cells.

Young employees are packed with honey and hung in chains close the building site. This is what we call festooning, and it's really incredible to see.

Festooning bees are also hanging in strings to make honeycombs.

If you have a hive that builds a comb, be very cautious when performing checks. You might be able to see this in the operation of your own hive.

The need for abundance of honey is another reason why feeding may encourage honey bees to construct a comb.

Our excess sugar water will assist to maintain the colony provided with a steady supply of food.

Now we know the three main variables that need to be addressed in order to encourage honey bees to construct a comb.

They must be in need of it, have hot weather and have plenty of meals available.

5 TIPS FOR MAKING HONEYCOMB BEES

1 Optimal Time of Year for Building Comb The time of year can affect how easy it is to get your bees out of the comb. Spring is a moment of natural upheaval.

Colonies feel the desire to boost the population and the potential swarm.

Therefore, it will be simpler to get your bees to create a basis (of building a comb) in the spring.

Try to use your foundation frames early in the year and save a few frames for later emergencies.

Is it difficult to remove the comb later in the year? Of course it's not. If the 3 requirements have been met, the bees will draw the comb.

In my knowledge, however, it is much more hard to encourage honey bees to construct comb after the first of July.

If I need frames constructed out, I'm going to work to get that completed before mid-Summer.

2 Feed Your Bees The Right Sugar Mix To Encourage Wax Production

Feeding your bees will encourage them to remove the comb. Even if the flow of nectar is on, most colonies will use the feeder at night or on rainy days.

If you are feeding your bees for comb construction reasons, use a 1:1 proportion of sugar to water.

This proportion simulates natural nectar and is more probable to result in fresh combs.

No, the honey stored in the hive does not seem to have the same impact. It's a fresh product coming in that stimulates the bees.

But you're not supposed to supply your bees when your honey supers are on, okay? Right! Right! Right! Honey produced from sugar water is not really honey.

However, if you add a super basis, you could feed your bees a little bit. This could offer them a boost to get began.

Understand that you might end up with a little sugar water in your honey super.

3 Baiting Up to Encourage Honey Bees to Build Comb in New Box If you have a colony that seems unwilling to move up to a fresh box, you may attempt "baiting up."

You bring the complete honeycomb frame out of the snakes ' cabinet and combine it with the base frame.

This may encourage the bees to migrate up to the next box.

There is no harm in doing this. Keep in mind, however, that if you handled mites with that picture in the bees portion of the cabinet, you may not want to eat it.

Beekeepers who use this technique should go home in a couple of weeks and move them back.

4 Swarms Love Building Comb If you capture a honey bee swarm, that's a wonderful chance to get a fresh comb. The employees in the swarm are prepared to make a comb for their fresh house.

They're going to quit the hive with wax glands willing to go! Once the swarms begin to draw the comb, they will often proceed as soon as you supply them.

This may be an chance to draw a few extra frames for subsequent use.

5 Young employees are the best ones to make honeycombs when you are creating divisions or regenerating a nest, maintain in mind that you need a bunch of youthful employees to generate wax at a quick rate.

Put the base frames in the cabinet with the youngest employees to see the finest comb manufacturing.

5 Tips To Encourage Bees To Draw Comb

Time of year Spring is the best way to feed your insects 1:1 sugar water!

Bait up to encourage expansion use swarms to construct comb to maintain a bunch of young adult bees We beekeepers enjoy our bees and want to do everything we can to assist. It's essential to note that we're managing bees, but we're not controlling them.

Our objective is to operate with the natural trends of the colony of honey bees.

If it's Spring, and you've got a good hive of bees, they're supposed to construct a comb when they're prepared.

And, it's not going to harm to make sure you maintain that feeder complete.

If you have excess beeswax after the honey harvest, it can be used for a lot of fun projects.

WARRE HIVE

WHAT IS A WARRE HIVE?

A Warre hive is a vertical top bar hive that uses bars instead of frames, usually with a wooden wedge or guide on the bars from which the bees build their own comb, just like they do in nature.

The Warre (pronounced: WAR-ray) hive is named after its inventor, French monk Abbé Émile Warré. He studied hundreds of different hive styles and settled on this one as the most ideal for bees and beekeeper. His design focused on simplicity, ease of management, and mimicry of honeybees' ideal natural environment. This hive is a vertically stacking top bar hive that incorporates natural comb and the retention of nest scent and heat. We've used these hives since 2008 and find them to be the most hands-off of any hive design.

Why Use A Warre Hive?

Warre hives are ideally suited for the beekeeper looking for a low-cost, low-maintenance hive design. With a Warre hive, there is no need to frequently inspect the colony, purchase an expensive honey extractor or use chemical-laden foundation. Management of Warre hives calls for adding extra boxes to the bottom of the stack (called nadiring), causing comb to be regularly harvested and cycled out of use. This prevents old comb from being reused and therefore ladened with environmental and agricultural chemicals and toxins.

In our mind the Warre hive is the ultimate design for natural, chemical-free beekeeping, and we've had tremendous success with our own Warres with little to no maintenance.

Advantages of using Warre hives

- Ideal for hands-off beekeepers
- Simple management by the box rather than by the comb
- Lighter boxes
- Optional windows
- Foundationless

History Of Warre Hives

Abbe Emile Warre developed the Warre hive over 50 years of research, culminating in what he liked to call "The People's Hive" in the early 1950s. He studied over 300 hive designs, ranging from straw skeps to the modern Langstroth hive, analyzing their ease of use and suitability for honey bees. He focused on simplicity, ease of management, and natural qualities including the building of natural comb (rather than pressed foundation) and the retention of nest scent and heat.

He frowned upon the invasive, tedious micromanagement of individual frames and combs as practiced by most beekeepers in his day. He found it optimal for bees and keeper that to manipulate the hive box by box only a couple times a year, rather than comb by comb every couple weeks. This is key to the beekeeping philosophy that corresponds with Warre hives, and it is a tremendous shift away from the common practices used today. Less bothering of bees means more productivity by and less disturbance to the colony.

Warre would typically add a couple empty boxes to the bottom of the hive in the spring and remove the top boxes from the hive (full of honey) in the fall. This allows for something few other hives offer: The continual cycle of new comb into and old comb out of the hive without the destruction of the precious brood chamber, as each year prior to winter the bees move the excess honey stores to the top of the hive. This removes the pesticide-laden comb from the hive every couple years, making for a healthier, happier colony.

How To Manage A Warre Hive

After using Langstroth, horizontal top bar and Warre hives, we love Warre hives for their simplicity, ease of management and success. We've had more success with Warre hives than any other hive design, and we don't think this is by chance.

BEE INSTALLATION

To install a bee package in a new Warre hive, start with 2 boxes, leaving any extras for holding a feeder. Set the the bottom up box with bars in place, and the top without.Place the queen cage on the bars of the bottom box and remove the cap exposing the hard candy. Shake the worker bees into the top box getting as many into the hive as possible. Then, lean the package near the entrance of the hive to encourage stragglers to move in. Replace the bars in the top box, then place the separator canvas, quilt box, and top it with the roof. Swarms can be installed with the same box configuration, without needing to place the queen cage.

MAINTENANCE HIVE CHECKS

Warre hives were designed to require minimal to no maintenance. Warre simply wanted beekeepers to add empty boxes to the bottom of the hive in the spring and harvest full boxes of honey off the top of the hive in the fall. Thus, Warre hives are meant to be managed by the box rather than by the comb.

Warre hives are meant to be expanded with the nadiring practice, by adding empty boxes to the bottom of the hive. The bees will generally build from the top down, and as their bottom most box becomes 80% full, an empty box can be added underneath. Then, excess honey will be harvested off the top of the hive.

Over the next couple months after installing your bees, monitor their growth by tilting the bottom box forward. If you see the bottom box filling with comb you can add another box or two accordingly. As fall arrives, check the bottom boxes for comb if they are empty you can remove them until the colony is down to 2-3 boxes.

Note: Bees will attach comb to the side walls of hive boxes since they do not have a 4 sided frame. This requires a sharp L-shaped tool to detach the comb.Our ultimate hive tools were designed for this purpose.They may also connect the comb from a top box to the top bars of the box below. This must be disconnected before lifting boxes off one another to avoid comb breakage, and can be done by cracking the propolis seal on all 4 corners, and then running a piano wire or guitar string between the boxes.

HONEY HARVEST

If you have been managing your hive by the box, rather than the individual combs, you will want to harvest by the box as well. This will require clearing bees out of the box to be harvested. You can do this by using a bee escape board. Place the board between the honey supers and the boxes you'd like to leave for the bees. Wait a couple days, especially as nights are getting cooler, and the bees will gradually move out of the supers, unable to find their way back up through the escape!

You can then remove the honey super from the hive and take out the top bars. Cut the comb from the top bars (our Ultimate Hive Tool is great for this), crush it up and strain using a mesh bag. Our Bucket Strainer System streamlines this process for a simple honey harvest.

Note: I don't recommend harvesting any honey in the first season, instead you should leave all of it for the bees and hope for a surplus next season!

Can Bees Recognize You?

Going about their day-to-day business, bees have no need to be able to recognise human faces. Yet in 2005, when Adrian Dyer from Monash University trained the fascinating insects to associate pictures of human faces with tasty sugar snacks, they seemed to be able to do just that. But Martin Giurfa from the Université de Toulouse, France, suspected that that the bees weren't learning to recognise people.

"Because the insects were rewarded with a drop of sugar when they chose human photographs, what they really saw were strange flowers. The important question was what strategy do they use to discriminate between faces," explains Giurfa. Wondering whether the insects might be learning the relative arrangement (configuration) of features on a face, Giurfa contacted Dyer and suggested that they go about systematically testing which features a bee learned to recognise to keep them returning to Dyer's face photos.

The team publish their discovery that bees can learn to recognise the arrangement of human facial features on 29 January 2010 in the Journal of Experimental Biology at http://jeb.biologists.org.

Teaming up with Aurore Avargues-Weber, the team first tested whether the bees could learn to distinguish between simple face-like images. Using faces that were made up of two dots for eyes, a short vertical dash for a nose and a longer horizontal line for a mouth, Avargues-Weber trained individual bees to distinguish between a face where the features were cramped together and another where the features were set apart. Having trained the bee to visit one of the two faces by rewarding it with a weak sugar solution, she tested whether it recognised the pattern by taking away the sugar reward and waiting to see if the bee returned to the correct face. It did.

So the bees could learn to distinguish patterns that were organised like faces, but could they learn to "categorize" faces? Could the insects be trained to classify patterns as face-like versus non-face like, and could they decide that an image that they had not seen before belonged to one class or the other?

To answer these questions, Avargues-Weber trained the bees by showing them five pairs of different images, where one image was always a face and the other a pattern of dots and dashes. Bees were always rewarded with sugar when they visited the face while nothing was offered by the non-face pattern. Having trained the bees that 'face-like' images gave them a reward, she showed the bees a completely fresh pair of images that they had not seen before to see if the bees could pick out the face-like picture. Remarkably they did. The bees were able to learn the face images, not because they know what a face is but because they had learned the relative arrangement and order of the features.

But how robust was the bees' ability to process the "face's" visual information? How would the bees cope with more complex faces? This time the team embedded the stick and dot faces in face-shaped photographs. Would the bees be able to learn the arrangements of the features against the backgrounds yet recognise the same stick and dot face when the face photo was removed? Amazingly the insects did, and when the team tried scrambling real faces by moving the relative positions of the eyes, nose and mouth, the bees no longer recognised the images as faces and treated them like unknown patterns.

So bees do seem to be able to recognise face-like patterns, but this does not mean that they can learn to recognise individual humans. They learn the relative arrangements of features that happen to make up a face like pattern and they may use this strategy to learn about and recognize different objects in their environment.

What is really amazing is that an insect with a microdot-sized brain can handle this type of image analysis when we have entire regions of brain dedicated to the problem. Giurfa explains that if we want to design automatic facial recognition systems, we could learn a lot by using the bees' approach to face recognition.

CONCLUSION

Honeybees provide a wide range of products and facilities (pollination) to human society and the ecosystem. Across the globe, bees are supporting millions of livelihoods while also enriching the ecosystem. Beekeeping is an significant undertaking for rural groups and linked to agricultural and horticultural manufacturing. Although the district of Uttara Kannada has over 60 per cent of its land under forest cover and about 15 per cent under agriculture, the manufacturing of honey is far below its anticipated capacity. The case study found that apiculture could be raised to a much more lucrative undertaking needing small capital investment and high-yield skilled labor compared to other rural employment and poverty reduction programs. We have taken into consideration the static efficiency of apiculture communities, which had played a crucial part in raising consciousness and profitability of science apiculture in their early days, helping individuals to set up apiary facilities in their households and helping to market the products. There are currently several individual entrepreneurs in the district who have noticed the significance of beekeeping, in a consumer society where there is a continuous and growing market demand for honey as a health food, as medicine, for use in confectionaries, in the pharmaceutical industry, and so on.

Kind reader,

Thank you very much. I hope you enjoyed the book.

Can I ask you a big favor?

I would be grateful if you would please take a few minutes to leave me a gold star on Amazon.

Thank you again for your support.

Andrew McDeere

Printed in Great Britain
by Amazon